MW01205782

The Pen and The Key

*50th Anniversary Anthology
of Pacific Northwest Writers*

The Pen and The Key

50th *Anniversary Anthology of Pacific Northwest Writers*

edited by Nigel Loring

selected by Pacific Northwest Writers Association

74th Street Productions   Seattle, Washington

Copyright © 2005 by 74th Street Productions, LLC

The Pen and The Key: 50th Anniversary Anthology of Pacific Northwest Writers

Foreword © 2005 Ann Rule
Cities of Gold © 2005 Kathleen Alcalá
Leaving Yesler © 2005 Peter Bacho
The Case for the Arts and Humanities, That Shadowy Figure © 2005 Marvin Bell
Facing Down the Monster © 2005 Terry Brooks
You Never Can Tell if the Water is Too Deep © 2005 Stella Cameron
Guess Who's Coming to Town! © 2005 Meg Chittenden
Dinner with Vlad, Vlad and Arturo Under the Stars © 2005 Robert Ferrigno
Born to Write? © 2005 Elizabeth George
Hollenbeck's First Rule of Medicine © 2005 Phyllis A.M. Hollenbeck, MD
Signore Bianco © 2005 J.A. Jance
The Loyal Order of Beasts © 2005 Kay Kenyon
The Kettle Boils—Out Pours a Novel © 2005 Bharti Kirchner
Madras © 2005 Craig Lesley
Bridget's Kitchen © 2005 Mark Lindquist
Another Time © 2005 Don McQuinn
Among the Shadows, Rule of Thumb © 2005 Fred Melton
Greatest Hero Ever © 2005 James Molnar
Passing Through © 2005 Marjorie Reynolds
F-150, Sleeping Apples © 2005 Daniel W. Sconce
Stay © 2005 Anna Sheehan
The Faithful Wife © 2005 Indu Sundaresan
The Yoke © 2005 Stephen John Walker
Calling the Roll © 2005 Shawn Wong

First Edition, August 2005
1   2   3   4   5   6   7   8   9

Library of Congress Cataloging-in-Publication Data
The pen and the key : 50th anniversary anthology of Pacific Northwest Writers
from the Pacific Northwest Writers Association/edited by Nigel Loring; selected by
   Pacific Northwest Writers Association.
   p. cm

ISBN 0-9655702-5-8

   1. Short stories, American—Northwest, Pacific
I. Loring, Nigel.

PS570.P46 2005   813´.010832795
            QB105-700014
Library of Congress Control Number: 2005925987

ACKNOWLEDGEMENTS

Pacific Northwest Writers Association (PNWA), a not-for-profit organization dedicated to developing writing talent from pen to publication, thanks these contributing authors who have supported the organization in the past and have donated their work to this commemorative project.

The printing of this book, made possible by The Boeing Company, is gratefully acknowledged.

This book is dedicated to Pacific Northwest Writers Association volunteers that include all past and present members of the Board of Trustees; selfless contest category chairs, readers, conference assistants, and respected authors; regional writing associations; and others who have sustained and expanded PNWA's dream.

Sharyn L. Bolton, President
(2004-2005)

CONTENTS

WRITING ABOUT WRITING

EMERGING WRITERS

FOREWORD

In my office, I have any number of large green plastic bins where I store research materials, old newspaper clippings, photographs of crime scenes and criminals, rough drafts of book manuscripts, mementos, receipts for the IRS, *and* old calendars. The calendars have turned out to be real treasures. Never someone who could stop to write in a diary or a journal, I save my calendars to remind myself where I've been and what I was doing. A scribbled notation evokes a detailed memory for me, some good and some disturbing. Some remind me of times in my life when every day was filled with an obligation or two, and it makes me tired just to look at them! Most of the jottings bring back good times.

My '70s calendars reflect the fads of those years three decades ago: orange and avocado green designs, big daisies, and stylized portraits of children with huge dark eyes. In my calendars' "Januarys," and in the third or fourth week of their "Julys," I have written "Pacific Northwest Writers' Conference!" I didn't need to embellish on that; my recollection of those times is crystalline.

What more wonderful place could there be for a fledgling writer than to be part of the Pacific Northwest Writers Association? I don't even remember now how I heard about this organization. I suspect it was in one of the magazines published for writers—either *The Writer* or *Writers' Digest*. I wasn't sure what you had to do—or be—to join. But I wanted very much to be part of it.

The summer conferences have always been my favorites. Four days in July where beginners could actually talk to publishers, editors and literary agents, where we could meet other writers and talk about our hopes and our frustrations as we learned from the experts about the mysteries of becoming *published* writers!

I do recall that it took a lot of courage for me to go —alone—to my first Pacific Northwest Writers Conference in the early seventies. It was the summer conference, and I didn't know anyone else who was attending. I certainly didn't know any of the speakers listed—although I recognized some of the names because they were *famous*.

As so many of the conferences were, my first was held at Pacific Lutheran University in Parkland, Washington, and attendees were staying at Nendel's Motel on Interstate 5. I got there about five, and I stayed in my room all evening while I occasionally heard laughter from rooms down the hall. I didn't know until the next day that those celebrants in the Hospitality Room had left an invitation for me at the front desk— one that I never got because the desk clerk put it in the wrong box.

Sitting alone in my room, unaware that I *had* been invited to the cocktail party down the hall, I felt like an impostor. After five years of nothing but rejection slips, I had finally sold a few things: three $35 articles to *The Seattle Times*' Sunday Magazine, and I'd been the editor of the *Baby Diaper Service Newsletter*. I'd even had a near-miss with *Inside Detective Magazine*, but, in the end, they didn't buy a piece I'd written about a murdered revenue agent because I couldn't get his relatives to sign releases. But I certainly wasn't selling consistently to any national magazine, and didn't think the members of PNWA would consider me an accomplished author.

Thank goodness, that was the first and only time I ever felt left out by my fellow writers. I soon learned that the PNWA welcomes everyone, probably because all of us have known more than our share of rejection in the cold printed notes we got from editors who felt our cherished manuscripts were "Not right for us at this time," "Not the material our publication is looking for," or "Just didn't meet our requirements."

If we were really lucky, we got a scribbled "Sorry" on the bottom of the standard rejection, or even a "Try us again." So being accepted into the circle at my initial Pacific Northwest Writers Conference was balm to my fragile ego. Today, thirty years later, I remember the early days and realize how much they meant to my career and how many friends the conference brought into my life, friends who are still with me. Many of Zola Helen Ross's writing students had worked hard to help the PNWA survive in the early years, and there were others who had laid the groundwork. Meg Chittenden, Donna Anders, Don McQuinn, Jeannie Okimoto, Anne Combs, Sheri Short, Archie Satterfield, Amos Wood, Gladys Nelson, Walt Morey and Dayton Hyde are some of the first names I learned, and I was vastly impressed.

Although it may be apocryphal, I heard that Jean Auel had been sitting at a panel at the conference when she was notified that she had been offered a contract with a huge advance for *Clan of the Cave Bear*! Whether it happened just that way or not, Jean was a shining example of what *could* happen.

The first *real* author I can remember hearing speak during a panel at Pacific Lutheran University was Lois Duncan, who had traveled from Albuquerque to attend. I sat way in the back, content to breathe the same air with published writers. Lois talked about how she helped support her children by writing true confession stories, and of her current career where she had blossomed into a very popular young-adult author.

I think the most important thing the conference offered was inspiration and encouragement. And Lois's talk certainly did that. If she could do it, I thought, then maybe I could, too. Since I had never actually known a published writer, it was essential for me to see one in person. And now I had.

For many years, our conference attendees bounced from the Rodeway Inn to Nendel's Motel to the Sherwood Inn. You never knew who you might meet. Most of us from those early days still talk about how excited we were when the PNWA's conference was just weeks away. One summer, there were *two* editors from *Cosmopolitan* sitting by the Nendel's pool, and there were New York City agents who were willing to take on a few new clients.

The conference cocktail parties in the lounges of these motels were packed full of people who balanced wine in plastic glasses, hors d'oeuvres, and, in the old days, cigarettes. If you could get your thoughts organized in a succinct way, you could pitch them to an editor or an agent. It wasn't easy over the din of voices, but a lot of us managed.

I met Len Dowty, the Articles Editor of *Good Housekeeping* that way, and I got an assignment from him, the first of several. That still seems miraculous to me, but why else would editors and agents attend writers' conferences if not to find writers?

And that is the second most important aspect of the

PNWA organization. If writers are basically talented and stubborn enough to hang in there despite dozens of rejection slips, I believe absolutely that they will eventually see their words in print. Often, all it takes is meeting someone in a position to make that happen. When that occurs, it can be serendipitous.

A few years later, after I had become the Northwest stringer for five fact-detective magazines, I became a presenter on a panel myself. That was a heady feeling for me, but I realize now it is part of the PNWA process of evolution. Those of us who came in as green and untested hopefuls moved on to share what we had learned in a school of sometimes *very* hard knocks.

After my first stint on a panel, an editor from *The Reader's Digest* who was also one of the speakers stopped me on the PLU campus. For some reason, he always called me "Old Ann Rule,"—even though I was in my middle thirties at the time.

"Old Ann Rule," he said, "Of everyone I've met here, I think you're going to make it because you just won't give up, and you're not a bad writer, either."

Only another struggling author can appreciate what his words meant to me.

Even at the Pacific Northwest Writers conferences, it isn't all inspiration and acceptance, however. One of my pet peeves has always been editors who seem to enjoy being doomsayers. They are the speakers who toss out impossible statistics: "There are only one-half of one percent of all writers in the United States who are making their livings from writing."

I could have agreed with that since I was making about one or two cents a word, but I refused to do it. Looking at it the pessimistic editors' way, it seemed prudent for all of us to give up, and go back to cooking, gardening, and laundry. Or engineering or banking or the practice of medicine—anything we did before we realized we were writers. The essential point is that none of us could take that viewpoint seriously.

There are still speakers out there who are quick to discourage. Don't even listen to them. Even if that should be accurate, I always say, "Then *you* be in that percentage!" And it seems to me that that has always been the prevailing opinion in the PNWA.

Through these decades, so many of our members have risen through the ranks to become national bestsellers—everyone's secret goal, even when we may pretend it doesn't matter. Not one of the following Northwest authors had any special entree into the publishing world; they got there with talent, hard work, and, yes, luck: Terry Brooks, John Saul, Don McQuinn, Meg Chittenden, Donna Anders, Earl Emerson, Gregg Olsen, Jack Olsen, Jean Auel, J.A. Jance, Stella Cameron, Debbie Macomber, Elizabeth Stone, Aaron Elkins, April Christophersen, Jayne Ann Krentz, Jeannie Okimoto, Robert Ferrigno, Ridley Pearson, and more. And me, too.

Nothing is impossible, and dreams *are* realized.

The Pacific Northwest Writers Association has always been unusual in the diversity of its members. We are both male and female, all ages, all races, from every economic level, and with greater and lesser degrees of formal education. The one thing that unites us is a passionate, obsessive, unshakable need to write.

And there are as many genres represented among our members as there are reasons for writing: romance, literary novels, military novels, science fiction, true crime, true confessions, psychological suspense, humor, fantasy, medical research, horror, children's stories, young adult novels, poetry, plays, movies, radio, television, mysteries, "cozys," animal stories, textbooks, political analysis, exposes, short stories, pulp, articles, advertisements, publicity, commercials, songs and on and on and on.

It's always fascinating to meet fellow writers and learn about what they are working on.

Many of our PNWA members have contributed to this anthology, and their stories and essays illustrate a myriad of approaches to the written word. I thoroughly enjoyed reading them!

I am sure you will, too.

Ann Rule,
Seattle, Washington, November 2004

SIGNORE BIANCO

J. A. Jance

Evil prowls the unsuspecting streets and canals of Naples, Italy, where only Signore Bianco stands in the way of the murder of an innocent young girl. This hard-boiled detective may be only the neighborhood mutt, but it is his territory after all. He has marked it well, and unwelcome interlopers had best beware.

SIGNORE BIANCO'S TERRITORY was small but very interesting. It stretched from the *Calle del Paradiso* to *Calle del Ugonegher*, between *Canal Grande* and *Calle del Olio*. The best part was the vast square with three spacious wooden benches, *Campo San Silvestro*, where nannies pushing their charges could be counted on for a pat on the head at least, while the babies pointed and laughed at *Signore Bianco's* white tail, curled proudly up over his back. Why babies found his tail laughable was one of the mysteries of life that *Signore Bianco* could not understand.

It was his self-appointed job to patrol the area—the towering, broad canyons of Venice—always on the lookout for intriguing visitors—like the lovely peach poodle who tripped daintily across *Campo San Silvestro* with her high heeled mistress on their way to and from the *vaporetto*. *Signore Bianco* had once asked this delectable beauty what it was she and her mistress did every day just after the ringing of nine bells. She had returned *Signore Bianco's* polite inquiry with a scathing look and told him, "*Mi lasci in pace!*" which more or less meant she thought it was none of his business. One could not blame him for hoping, however.

His days were long. He started in the morning by paying a brief call on the two Pekinese, *Signora Fragola*, Madame Strawberry, and her delightful daughter, *Signorina Albicocca,* Miss Apricot. They lived in the busy *Ristorante San Silvestro*. The luckless *Signore Bianco* had often expressed his interest in Miss Apricot as well, but when he told her, "*Sono allupato,*" she told him "*Vai al diavolo,*" which was more or less what the poodle had told him but a little cruder.

Now that he knew neither of the Pekinese would ever be his lover, *Signore Bianco* had resigned himself to an easy friendship. When he saw them every morning, they were always eager to tell him who had come by the restaurant the previous night and especially about the ill-behaved mongrels, the *idioti imbicille,* who usually came from far away places like *Campo del Pescaria* where they evidently spent each and every day fighting it out with the seagulls over ill-smelling fish guts. And then there was the crazy Dalmation from *Campo San Polo,* an obnoxious, ugly brute, who seemed to think he was *Il Doge* himself.

Once ten o'clock came, *Signore Bianco* would sit and chat for a while with one of his old friends, the ancient, arthritic bulldog called Rocky, whose owner managed the Internet Café on *Calle del Ugonegher.* Together they would laugh about the strange foreigners and their odd accents, wonderfully aromatic shoes, and heavy backpacks, who came to sit at Rocky's master's funny looking machines which they poked eagerly with their busy fingers. Why people from so many places were all interested in those machines was another one of life's mysteries.

After Rocky and *Signore Bianco* had communed for a sufficient time, he would continue his rounds, treading through the neighborhood carefully so that one or more of the thoughtless people streaming around him didn't step on him. And then, when the *bandone*, the security grates, were folded back down over the shop windows, it was time for lunch. He would saunter back to his home, around the corner from *Café al Paradiso*. He would scratch on the door. His mistress would let him inside for a long afternoon nap on his soft rug, his *tappeto*, against the cool wall of the foyer.

"And so," she would ask him. "What have you been doing this morning, Snowball?"

Signore Bianco had no idea what that word meant, but it seemed like an undignified name for a detective of his importance and standing in the world. Not only that, his mistress never waited to hear his answer. Instead, the telephone would ring or she would start fixing her own lunch or turn on the stupid television set without even bothering to listen. It concerned him sometimes, that humans were so insensitive to the world around them, so oblivious as to what was truly important.

Late afternoons and evenings were *Signore Bianco's* favorite times of day. As the *cuoci*, the chefs in the restaurants prepared their evening fare, there were always good smells floating in the air. There were also the intriguing smells covering the ground with all their many mysteries waiting to be decoded. That was when the *turisti*—*gli Americani* with their strange bare legs and knobby knees and amazingly fragrant tennis shoes and *gli Tedeschi*, the Germans, with their sandals and sour smelling socks—would all congregate along the *Canal Grande* where they would perch in chairs along the walls of the cafes. There, like so many pigeons strung on a wire, they would sip their *espresso* and smoke their foul-smelling cigars while heavily laden gondolas came and went.

Sometimes *Signore Bianco* and the two Pekes would sit in the doorway of the restaurant and watch clumsy *turisti* scramble in and out of gondolas. Occasionally the three dogs would make small bets among themselves as to which of the drunken ones would fall into the water and have to be dragged out. And, of course, since the locals couldn't be bothered, the drunks always had to be rescued by fellow *turisti* who also ended up soaking wet. That was always good for a laugh.

It was the middle of May—too early for the worst of the tourist hordes to have descended on the broad avenues of Venezia—when *Signore Bianco* was summoned to his biggest and most difficult case. For someone who was only three hundred millimeters high, this case would prove to be a profound test of his detecting skills to say nothing of his *coraggioso*, his courage.

He was exceptionally tired that day. For some reason, a flock of foreign pigeons had descended on *Campo San Silvestro* early that morning, and *Signore Bianco* had worn himself out chasing them out of the square. That was, after all, an important part of his job. But when he lay down on his *tappeto* in the afternoon, he found he was restless and unable to sleep. Three times he sighed and rose and turned three times before lying down again, but still he found no comfortable position.

Signore Bianco arose two hours later from this fruitless attempt at a nap to find himself uncharacteristically cross and irritable and in the middle of an oppressively overcast afternoon. Finally, late in the day, a fierce thunderstorm rolled through the city. Echoing peels of thunder rumbled off building walls. Torrents of hard-driven rain sent unsuspecting tourists scurrying for cover. Locals, calm in the face of the furious storm, simply pulled their *umbrelle* out of bags and walked unscathed through the downpour. Meanwhile, drenched and disappointed *turisti* huddled in cafes and cursed the sky for delaying their walk to something called the *Duomo*, wherever that might be.

By the time his mistress let *Signore Bianco* out again, the rain was gone and the city smelled fresh and clean. There were still a few puddles here and there, but not enough to get your paws wet. He wandered the neighborhood, checking the pee-mail to see if one of his friends had left him a message. Or a joke. At *Café al Paradiso* the waiters were just finishing setting up their tables for dinner. That's when the trouble started. Being a dog, *Signore Bianco* smelled it long before he heard or saw it.

Everyone, even humans, know that people have their own distinctive smells. Some of it is, of course, entirely artificial—flowery scents or spicy ones that come from *profumeria* that are designed to conceal things like sweat. Then there are medicinally strong minty smells that supposedly disguise bad teeth and bad breath. But there are no deodorants that can conceal the terrible stench of an evil man's soul. To *Signore Bianco's* finely tuned nostrils, the awful odor was unmistakable.

It was not the easy *e cosi* attitude of the gypsies whose wily sense of larceny generally means little more than 'your watch is my watch.' No, this was something far more sinister, and as it drew closer, *Signore Bianco* realized that the awful smell was accompanied by another more subtle one, the flowery, delicate scent of a woman's perfume. That meant there were two people, a man and a woman, walking together.

Before the invisible couple came into view, however, *Signore Bianco's* sensitive ears were assailed by a sound that was almost as disturbing as the terrible odor. The detective instantly recognized the sound emitted by a pair of ill-fitting shoes, but this time the noise was appalling. It sounded as though whoever was approaching was squashing one useless Chihuahua after another with every deliberate step.

With his stiff white hair standing at attention, *Signore Bianco* stared as the couple rounded the corner. The man was tall and burly, wearing a camera on a leather strap around his neck. His broad chest was covered by one of those vulgar Hawaiian shirts favored by Americans. The woman was young, stylishly dressed, and definitely Italian. She was chatting eagerly on the phone, telling someone that she would see her later.

Using a firm hand on the young woman's slender waist, the man guided her up to the menu posted outside the *Café al Paradiso* where they paused long enough to peruse the listings. That in itself was an instant giveaway of the man's national origin. Of all the *touristi* wandering the streets of Venice, only the Americans consistently eat at such an appallingly early hour.

Signore Bianco glanced around him to see if anyone else had noticed the approaching danger, but no one had. *Signore Bianco* counted the wait staff of the café among his many friends. As he made his evening rounds, he often found them standing outside the restaurant, smoking cigarettes and chatting. The head waiter especially, a jovial man named Roberto, was usually good for a treat or two, but this time, rather than driving the intruder away, Roberto welcomed the man warmly. After exchanging a few words, the head waiter ushered the couple to one of the outdoor tables.

That was more than *Signore Bianco* could stand. And, even though it was far outside the realm of civilized behavior, he stationed himself as near to the evil man's noisy shoes as possible and began to bark—furiously. The young woman had finished her conversation and put her cell phone down. She seemed to find *Signore Bianco's* bark amazingly funny. She laughed while the man scowled. Roberto hissed, "*Basta*—enough!" And "*Sparisca*—get lost!"

But *Signore Bianco* didn't stop. He kept right on barking. Finally, one of the kitchen helpers appeared with a broom and chased him away. That was astonishing. Not only did Roberto and the others ignore *Signore Bianco's* warning of impending disaster, they actually attacked him—drove him out like a common mongrel with no business being on the street.

Faced with such undignified treatment, a lesser dog might have given up and crept home with his tail between his legs. Not *Signore Bianco*. He stationed himself just around the corner from the restaurant where he was out of sight, but close enough to observe the goings on.

All through dinner—from the *aperitivo* through the *antipasti misti, primo piatto, secondo piatto* to the *dolci*, the young woman chatted vividly, talking about what she was studying in school and what she intended to do when she finished her education. The man, who was much older than she, appeared to be listening intently, but *Signore Bianco* knew he was not. There was something else at work here. It was only when the young woman excused herself to visit the WC that *Signore Bianco* realized what it was.

It was still so early that no other diners were seated at any of the other tables. Finding himself alone, the man reached into his pocket extracted something, and poured it into the young woman's drink. This time *Signore Bianco* knew better than to attempt to bark a warning. It would have served no purpose. No one would have paid any attention. Worse yet, it was possible that Roberto would summon *Signore Bianco's* mistress on the telephone and tell her to come and fetch her bothersome dog.

And so, still staring at his target, *Signore Bianco* huddled even closer to the wall and tried to make himself invisible.

When the young woman returned to the table and resumed sipping her drink, it was soon apparent that she was no longer in control of herself. Her words came out more slowly, as though she were just learning to speak.

She seemed suddenly very sleepy, or else very drunk. The man rose abruptly and went into the restaurant, probably to pay the bill. Seeing his chance, *Signore Bianco* hurried to the table and whined appealingly, hoping to entice the young woman away before the man returned.

It didn't work. Instead of taking the hint, she simply gazed at *Signore Bianco* stupidly and didn't move. He was still there when the man returned. Seeing the dog, the man aimed a vicious kick at *Signore Bianco's* unprotected ribs. Fortunately, he was quick enough to dodge out of the way. The kick connected, but without nearly as much damage as it would have done had it not been for his quick, evasive maneuver. Still, with an amazingly authentic yelp— one that sounded for the world as though he had been gravely injured—*Signore Bianco* limped around the corner and disappeared once more into the sheltering shadow of a doorway.

From that concealed vantage point he watched the couple walk toward *Canal Grande*. There was no longer any question of the girl chatting amiably as they walked. In fact, she could barely walk at all. Her legs moved from time to time, but woodenly, like a clumsy marionette, and it was the man with his arm flung protectively around her shoulder who was pulling the strings.

There was no time to raise an alarm, and no point, either. Who would believe him? No, only *Signore Bianco* realized that the young woman was in terrible danger. If she was to be saved, it was up to him.

He followed them discreetly, keeping to the shadows. As they passed *Ristorante San Silvestro,* he looked longingly inside, hoping for a glimpse of one or the other of the two Pekes. Not that either one of them could have helped him, but at least *Signore Bianco* might have told them what was happening and he wouldn't have been so alone. But neither *Signora Fragola* nor her daughter were anywhere in sight.

Walking quickly now, the man hustled the increasingly wooden young woman past the shuttered storefronts on the *Ponte Rialto*. People hurrying past them in either direction were too intent on going home to their own dinners to pay any attention to the man and his obviously drunken date. Only *Signore Bianco* kept them in sight.

Venice is a busy city—a packed and crowded city—with no wide tracts of vacant space. Still, there are places one is better off not visiting at night—little nooks and crannies and trash laden courtyards where bad things might happen and where the crime might not be discovered until much later.

Signore Bianco was worried—for the girl, yes, but also for himself. This was unknown territory. He had been on the far side of the Rialto Bridge before on occasion, but only on a lead and with his mistress when she went out intent on buying something at one of the more fashionable shops. As the man hurried on, the dog, trotting to keep up, knew it was possible for even he—expert detective that he was—to become hopelessly lost in the maze of circling alleys and darkened thoroughfares.

Crossing one of the smaller canals, the young woman's legs gave way completely. The man simply lifted her up—hefting her easily as though she weighed nothing—and carried her along. He turned into a courtyard and then went through an arch where, a few meters away, the black water of that same canal glinted before him. It was only when *Signore Bianco* turned to follow them that he realized the walkway ended a little way beyond the arch where it came up against the unyielding side of a small and ancient church.

And it was there, with bare walls on two sides and with the canal on another that the man dropped his load, letting the young woman fall to the ground as though she were a gunny sack of potatoes being dropped off a handcart outside *Café al Paradiso's* kitchen's door. The force of the fall brought the young woman's breath out of her chest in a powerful whoosh, but after that she made no other sound, nor did she make any effort to move.

Standing frozen just inside the archway, *Signore Bianco* waited silently to see what would happen. For a moment nothing did. The man seemed to be standing over her, considering what he should do next. Then, with a single powerful motion, he reached down and swiped his hand across her still body. The hand came away holding a fistful of torn clothing. He stepped back a few meters and stood still with his feet wide apart, as if admiring his handiwork.

Through the man's spread legs, *Signore Bianco* caught a glimpse of the now half naked girl lying limp and unmoving on the ground. Then, to the dog's astonishment, he was almost blinded by a sudden flash. In the few dark disorienting seconds that followed *Signore Bianco* realized that man had used the camera around his neck to take the girl's picture. That was followed by the inevitable knowledge that if the man had stooped so low as to take a picture of the girl in all her helpless nakedness, then what was to follow would be that much worse.

There was not a moment to lose. Without making a sound, *Signore Bianco* hurtled down the narrow bank. The man was standing over the girl with his belt unfastened and with his pants halfway down when *Signore Bianco* plowed into the small of his back. He was a small dog, but momentum made him a powerful force. His blow caught the man off balance. He staggered toward the water. Half a step away, he tripped over his half-mast trousers and tumbled into the canal. He bobbed to the surface almost immediately, choking and coughing. With flailing arms, he made toward the bank. His fingers grasped the edge, and he might have pulled himself out, but *Signore Bianco* was there, too. His sharp teeth clamped around the man's fingers, biting down with all his might. His bite drew blood and a screech of panicked protest.

Again and again the man tried to climb out of the water. Again and again, *Signore Bianco* drove him back. And then—it could have been the fifth time he bit him or the tenth—the man fell suddenly still. In the dim light, *Signore Bianco* saw his eyes roll back into his head, and then he sank out of sight. In the stricken silence that followed, *Signore Bianco* heard voices. He was grateful to think that someone was coming, but then, still shaking with effort, he realized that the sound was coming from the girl's telephone which had fallen out of her clothing and gone skidding across the walkway.

"Gina," a woman's voice was saying more and more desperately. "Gina, is that you? What's happening? Are you all right? Who was that screaming? Gina?"

Signore Bianco went over and sniffed the girl's still body. She was breathing and snoring both. Sitting on his haunches, he waited over her until he heard the sound of a police boat nosing its way up the canal. He stayed long enough to see one of the officers leap off the boat, then he melted into the shadowy archway and then slowly, sniffing to locate his own scent, he made his way back home.

It took a long time. *Signore Bianco* was tired and sore. His body felt stiff, as though it had been through a war, as indeed it had. His ribs ached and so did his jaws—from all the biting. His bruised nose didn't seem to work with all its usual efficiency. Hours passed before he finally crossed *Ponte Rialto* and was back in familiar territory. By then it was late, very late. *Café al Paradiso* was closed up tight for the night, with the tables empty and with the outside chairs chained together. As soon as *Signore Bianco* scratched feebly at the door, his mistress flung it open wide.

"Oh, *Pallina de Neve*," she cried, picking him up and hugging him to her. "Oh, Snowball, you bad, bad boy! Where have you been? I've been so worried. And what is this? It looks like blood! Is it? Are you hurt? What has happened to you, *mio povero cucciolo*, my poor puppy?"

Signore Bianco would have been glad to tell her, but as usual, his mistress didn't stay still long enough to hear any of his answers. She hurried away to get a wet cloth and a towel with which to clean him.

Lying on his tapetto, *Signore Bianco* was glad enough to be home, but as he drifted off to sleep, it occurred to him that he would have appreciated a somewhat more dignified and heroic welcome.

ANOTHER TIME

Don McQuinn

WWII changed the geopolitical fabric of the entire planet, but nowhere was its effect more profound than on the ingrained racial attitudes of America, both north and south. The changes wrought in the turbulent '60s were born in the late '40s. Progress continues to be measured one soul at a time.

THEY CAME ON the train, over two hundred of them, stepping down the coach stairs into the full weight of East Texas sunshine with an animal wariness. Only a handful of locals were watching. Tommy John and I were the only kids. We'd been walking the tracks because we were going fishing and we hoped we'd get lucky and hop a freight to the fishing hole. Jumping off could be scratchy, but we were young; cuts and bruises were our daily portion.

An unscheduled passenger train stopping in our little town meant a troop train. We ran to the landing. Soldiers had cigarettes. Tailor-mades. Kids either smoked roll-your-owns made of Bull Durham or Bugler or we stole from our parents. Mine smoked Philip Morris; stealing them wasn't hardly worth the effort and absolutely not worth the risk. The chance to bum a smoke off a soldier—maybe even buy a whole pack—was not to be missed.

Our first look at the men off-loading changed all that. They were different. Curiosity pulled their attention this way and that, but there was something about that curiosity that raised the hair on my neck If you made eye contact, they looked into you, not just at you. The uniforms were all wrong, too, especially the hats. And they were dirty. Anyone traveling by train got dirty. Texas summer heat did awful things to the inside of the coaches. If you wanted to breathe, you opened the windows. Once you did, though, all the smoke and dust and ash in the world blew in. These men looked especially hard used. Their clothes were the mess you'd expect, but more than that, most were stained and some were even torn.

Tommy John said, "That's the raggedy-assedest soldiers I ever saw. You reckon they were on a train that wrecked, or something?"

While he was saying it, one of the soldiers yelled at another one. Right then I remembered all the talk of the past few weeks.

"Prisoners," I said. From the corner of my eye, I saw Tommy John swivel my way. I kept my attention on the strangers. "Germans. That's the Germans."

The Army built a camp for them not far from our farm. It'd been standing empty long enough for everyone to get used to it and the bored guards hanging around. As soon as Mama heard about the place she made it clear we kids weren't ever going anywhere near it. This might be my only chance to actually see a real German.

Tommy John said, "Shit fire, I believe you're right. Look there at the first car and the last one. They got to be the guards."

Two trios of American soldiers carrying shotguns watched the prisoners. The Germans didn't ignore the guards, but they didn't look right at them, either. It was like they were trying to wish them away. They certainly didn't look afraid. They'd lost and been captured. That didn't mean they meant to roll over and show their bellies.

The guards sort of stood around, the shotguns held easy across their bodies. Directly, one of them—a sergeant—said something to one prisoner and that one said something louder to the rest. In about five seconds just about every one was smoking.

Tommy John licked his lips. "You reckon it'd be all right to bum a cigarette off a German? The cigarettes are American; I saw Luckies."

"Hell, no. They're enemies. You don't ask enemies for nothing."

"They don't look like enemies. Yonder—that one, with the big tear in his britches—looks just like Mr. Martin."

We both laughed. Mr. Martin was the least-liked teacher in our school, a 4-F in the draft who paid way too much attention to the young women of the area, and not just the single ones. I heard Dad one night tell Mama Mr. Martin had less chance of living through the war than anyone in the service. Mama said that was an un-Christian thing to say, and Dad told her Mr. Martin knew as much about Christ as a hog knows about a fiddle. Then they saw me listening and I was sent off to get my brothers and sisters to dinner.

I told Tommy John, "We might could get a smoke off a guard."

"You crazy?" Tommy John snorted. "You don't walk up to no shotgun guard. He'd put a load of double-ought buck through you quicker'n shit through a goose. We'd bury what was left of your skinny ass in a cigar box."

Whatever chance we had of addressing that matter further ended when the jeep rolled up. A mumble ran through the prisoners as they watched it park just past the station. When a lieutenant got out and stared at them, hands on hips, the mumble changed to a sort of sigh.

I knew instantly what that sound meant. To this day, that surprises me. I was a kid, barely sixteen, and knew as much about life as the average puppy, but when I heard that exhalation I knew those men were acknowledging that they'd reached the final phase of a major event in their lives. Over the decades I've heard a sound of that nature only rarely, of course. Still, whenever I do, I'm that boy again, listening to inarticulate despair and relief coil around each other.

The American soldiers threw down their cigarettes— Tommy John and I both groaned at the length of the butts —and straightened up. The lieutenant headed for the three at the front passenger car. "C'mon," I said, "Let's get closer so we can hear."

I wish I could see us as we were, two kids with ridiculous nonchalance pretending to stroll through a scene that was literally historic. The civilians saw exactly what we were up to. Mrs. Cuthbert hissed at us like a snake. Damned fool Tommy John turned to say, "'Mornin', Miz Cuthbert. How are you today?"

Mrs. Cuthbert said, "Never mind that. Those men are Germans. Prisoners of war. Get you away from there."

I just hurried along like I hadn't heard. She was a nice enough lady. She just couldn't help herself. Knew what was best for everybody and would rather break a bone than not tell them so.

Talking to a sergeant and the other two guards, the lieutenant never gave any sign he was aware of us. His voice was low, indistinct. The guards were shaking their heads and frowning. When the lieutenant spun around to face us, Tommy John and I both yelped and jumped back. I recall that lieutenant's face now and he wasn't that much older than us. To a couple of country boys startled half out of their wits, however, he was Mars himself. His eyes were dark as coffee and he had a brittle way of talking that made his words crackle. He said, "I need somewhere with shade. These men are waiting for trucks. Can you show me a place?"

I spoke first. "The park. About a half mile." Tommy John pitched in. "Got a drinking fountain. For water. And benches. Toilets, too."

I hadn't thought of those things. To hear Tommy John talk, he was as dumb as dirt. If you listened to what he said, though, he was smarter than hell. Today he runs a huge ad agency and sounds so cultured it's enough to give an old friend fits.

Mayor Rowe showed up then, blowing hard, very official. My dad said his gut hung over his belt the way it did because the man was so full of himself there wasn't anyplace else for it to go. He glared at the lieutenant. "What're you going to do about this situation?" he said, jerking a thumb at the Germans.

The lieutenant was calm. "My prisoners will walk to your town park. These two young men will ride with me as guides. I need you to call the camp and tell them where to pick us up. Thank you."

It was all we could do to keep from running to the jeep. With us in the back, the lieutenant drove away at a walking pace. The Germans followed, the guards alongside like outriders driving a herd. We hadn't gone thirty yards when we jammed to a stop. One of the Germans was by himself, a step to the right of the head of the column, counting cadence. The Germans were marching.

The lieutenant bucked out of the car like a bull out of a rodeo chute. The next thing we knew, he was yelling at the single German: "*Nein!*" I'd read enough comic books to know that meant No. The Germans stumbled to a stop, all wide eyes and open mouths. The American guards weren't looking any better. Then the lieutenant shouted, "*Achtung!*"

The whole bunch went stiff as fenceposts. Roaring,

the lieutenant kept on. In German. It sounded awful. I asked Tommy John, "What's he saying?"

"How the hell do I know, dummy? Sounds like somebody beating a tree with a stick, don't it? Whatever it is, them ol' boys don't much like it."

As the lieutenant's voice dropped to a more regular level, the Germans sort of relaxed. Except for the single one. He was angry, his face as tight as a tick. That's when I realized he was the one the sergeant spoke to when the Germans first got off the train, so I knew he spoke some English. Either the lieutenant didn't know that or didn't care; he kept firing away in German. When he turned sideways, we could see his face, too. Those two men were enemies. No other word would touch it.

The lieutenant stepped away and gestured the American sergeant to him and gave him a few words, too. The sergeant's salute as the officer left was stiff as starch.

When the lieutenant got back in the jeep, I asked him what he said. He told me, "No marching. No cadence, no formation. The war's over for them. I told them they'll be treated well as long as they obey orders."

Tommy John said, "What'd you tell our sergeant? You were talking about that German who was marching the others, weren't you?"

A burning gaze made Tommy John squirm. Finally, the lieutenant said, "I told him to get his head out of his ass long enough to learn the difference between a German and a Nazi."

I said, "What is the difference?"

The lieutenant frowned, made a noise. "I'm not your teacher. Learn the way I did; watch." He started the jeep and waved our parade forward.

It was more fun than the law allows. By the time we reached the park, there was a crowd of at least a hundred people, some walking alongside the prisoners. The Germans were pretty nervous at first, but shortly they were sort of smiling at the folks who looked most friendly. It took a while for anyone to smile back. There never was any great warmth to it. After all, it wasn't all that long ago those men were trying to kill ours. No one was forgetting that.

Shade helps in East Texas, but it's no cure. When we stopped the lieutenant told us these Germans were Africa Corps, desert fighters. The humidity in this part of the world hit them hard. There was always a line at the drinking fountain. Mostly, though, they just sat and talked quietly. I watched the one that had counted cadence. He kept looking at me and Tommy John like he associated us with the lieutenant and he didn't like us any more than he liked him. To be honest with you, he scared me. Little by little, he drifted our way. When he'd catch one of us looking at him, he'd kind of smile, like he knew a secret.

I told Tommy John, "I believe that son of a bitch is trying to scare us."

"Doing a good job, too. I'm glad those guards are here."

I thought about leaving and it made me mad. The German couldn't be crazy enough to do anything to me or Tommy John and I knew he was pushing to see if we'd back up. I was damned if I would. I knew if I didn't Tommy John wouldn't either.

The trucks took hours to arrive. By then a few prisoners were even trying to talk to folks. A couple of ladies showed up with coffee and some cookies. The Germans were like kids, all smiles, really grateful. Our bad guy made it clear he didn't like any of it. The rest didn't pay much attention.

There were ten trucks. The drivers were all black, and when they stepped out of the cabs the crowd buzzed at the sight. The lieutenant had all the drivers report to him and he didn't waste words. "I sent word to the camp for you to come here hours ago. Explain."

The man in charge stepped forward. He was what

they called a tech sergeant. He said, "Never got no word, Lieutenant. A civilian asked the gate guard if the Germans in town was coming to our camp. Captain Bernard, he called the police. They said where you was and Captain Bernard say we get our asses moving. We here, sir."

"Nobody called the camp?"

"No, sir. I'm sure. We been sitting in them trucks, waiting. Didn't get no chow, nothing. You reckon we can get us a drink over yonder?"

"Go ahead."

Before the truck drivers could move somebody said, "No, they can't."

It was Mayor Rowe. His face was pinched shut, red as turkey wattles. People around him didn't look much happier. The lieutenant's surprise was funny. He had to work to get words out. "What did you say?"

Mayor Rowe drew himself tall as he could get. "That fountain's whites only, sir. Your drivers are colored. There's a colored honkytonk that way, down by the river."

Shock made me speak. "Mayor, the Germans been drinking there all afternoon. We're at war with them. Folks been giving them cookies and everything."

That got me a look that told me I'd hear about this for the rest of my life. I didn't care. He leaned closer, almost in my face. "Those are white men. The same laws apply to them as the rest of us."

The lieutenant said, "Just a God damned minute. Fucking krauts use your pissy little fountain and American soldiers can't? Are you crazy?"

I didn't think Mayor Rowe could get any redder. Actually, he didn't; he went sort of purple. When he talked, he squeaked. "You talk to me respectful. I'll report you."

"Report this, you stupid hick. My men drink anywhere they want. Who's going to stop us?"

Some of the drivers tightened up, the way men do when they're getting ready to do heavy lifting. The shotgun guards were paying close attention to the crowd. Tommy John and I started to pull back, but we bumped up against something. When we looked, the nasty German was looking down at us. He had that smile again.

I wasn't going to let anyone see me run. I saw Tommy John was as scared and stubborn as I was. We faced forward again.

The tech sergeant put a hand on the lieutenant's arm and said, "It's okay, sir. Don't make trouble for yourself. Please. You a good officer, sir; we don't want you should get in trouble over us." He didn't give the lieutenant a chance to argue. Instead, he hollered at the guards. "Load 'em up! Twenty to a truck. Leftovers get squoze in anywhere. On the double!"

Relief washed over the guards' faces as they went to work. The Germans, too. They didn't understand everything they'd just seen, but that sort of tension is contagious.

It should have ended right there, except little old Mayor Rowe couldn't let go. He crowded right up to the lieutenant. He said, "Just because there's a war on, people like you put on a uniform and think you can come here and tell us what to do. Agitators is what you are. You know why you Yankees got race riots and we don't? Niggers know their place down here. You and your damfool ways. Let anybody vote—niggers, Republicans, Communists— any damn' body. It ain't going to happen here, soldier boy. You don't like it, go back where you come from."

Behind me, the German said, "*Ja*" and everyone stared. He went on, "*Deutschland* same. *Nein schwartzer, nein Juden.*" Nobody said anything, so he tried again. "No nay-gur, no Jew."

Now the nasty secret smile was aimed at Mayor Rowe. You could see the mayor thinking about that, his eyes dancing like spit on a hot stove. Then he smiled back. It was thin, almost too quick to catch, but I saw it.

Whatever the lieutenant said wiped the German's face clean. He paled, blinked, and sprinted for the closest truck. I mean, he *ran*. The lieutenant didn't even watch

He barely finished speaking before concentrating on me. He almost whispered, like this was too important to share with anyone else. "You asked me how to tell the difference between a German and a Nazi, and I said you watch people. Remember?"

"Yes, sir."

"Good." That was it. He got in his jeep and left.

Within a year, I was gone, too, part of the war that brought the Germans to us. The camp was abandoned— torn down, in fact—when I finally came home. Dad said the Germans were no trouble. Just one escaped. Got caught two days later and sent elsewhere. I figured I knew which one that was.

I visited the park, remembering everything that happened that strange day. Closing my eyes I smelled the train—smoke on the prisoners' clothes, the sweat. I saw them, heard the roll and catch of their exotic language.

Mayor Rowe was dead. Tommy John, down to one leg, thanks to Japanese artillery, was in college, full of ambition.

More than anything else I remembered that lieutenant. Never even knew his name. He said he wasn't a teacher. Like hell. He taught me one of the most important things I know.

Some wars never end.

Passing Through

Marjorie Reynolds

Two young men visit their mother fourteen years after she abandoned them. It takes place in the Midwest in 1946, when life seemed simpler but human emotions remained the same.

FROM HIS TRUCK, Cal surveyed the empty gravel parking lot. The diner needed a coat of paint. Patches of bare wood pocked the clapboard, giving it the appearance of advanced leprosy. Four large windows faced the highway. Above them, a switched-off neon sign advertised HAROLD'S ALL-NITE DINER, a curiosity because the place didn't stay open all night. Maybe it did once, but his brother Mel had made a point of saying it opened at six o'clock in the morning.

"Looks closed to me," he said.

His brother Chet glanced at his watch. "Nah, it's about time." He gave the passenger door a shove and lowered his foot onto the running board. "Well, come on."

Cal slowly got out. This was a bad idea.

"Let's have a smoke out here first," he said.

Chet shrugged and reached in his shirt pocket for his Lucky Strikes.

They leaned against the battered fender of the green Dodge truck and puffed on the cigarettes. Animal odors from the nearby pasture overpowered any preview of breakfast that might have come from the diner.

A brand new '46 Packard Super Clipper whizzed by, its sleek blue fenders catching a glint of sun. Cal watched it disappear down the long straight highway.

Chet's gaze also tracked the shiny car. "How do you suppose some hayseed out here can afford an automobile like that?"

Cal flicked the ash off his cigarette. "Probably some fellow passing through on his way to Louisville."

"Yeah, I s'pose."

Cal glanced at the notch of sun on the eastern horizon. A light breeze brushed his bare arms, face and neck. Normally, early morning was his favorite time of day.

After a few more drags, Chet crushed the butt under his shoe and started toward the diner.

Cal held back. "How do you know she's here?"

Chet turned. "Mel said she'd be. Don't you think he knows?"

"Well, I don't understand why you want to see her."

"'Cause we're leaving again. We might not be coming back this direction for a long time."

"So, do you think she cares?"

She hadn't cared fourteen years ago when she locked him and Chet in the closet, took four-year-old Mel and left. Occasionally—not often, but when he had a fever or wasn't sleeping well—he sank again into claustrophobic darkness, smelled the damp mustiness of old coats and rubber boots and clawed the air, wheezing asthmatically, struggling frantically to get out, his heart slamming against his chest. If Chet hadn't been in there, pulling on him, begging him to stop, he might have scratched his fingernails to bloody stumps against that heavy walnut door.

So, when the judge took them out on the back porch of the courthouse, gave each of them a piece of hard candy and asked, "Who do you boys want to live with—your ma or your pa?" he had just shrugged and said, "Our pa, I guess. Ma didn't want us."

"She says she would have taken all three of you right then, but she was afraid she couldn't manage."

"We wouldn't have been no trouble."

"She was worried about feeding all you boys."

"Chet and me don't eat much."

The old white-haired judge smiled. "Well, I'm going to let you boys decide." He waited a moment. "All right, then. It'll be your pa, if you're sure."

Cal thought of the dark, dank closet, fixed his mouth in a tight line and said, "I'm sure."

The judge nodded, then peered at Chet, who was seven at the time. "How about you?"

Chet's brown eyes opened wider. "I want to go where Cal goes."

The judge awarded custody to their father, who earned a good living, even during the depression, but worked like a crazed man gambling it away.

Chet nodded toward the diner. "I want to see her. Aren't you curious?"

"No."

"Aw, come on. It won't take long, and besides I'm hungry. I'm not riding halfway across the State of Illinois without any food in my belly."

Cal trailed him into the diner. As they passed the long wooden counter, the eight chrome stools and the silent jukebox, he smelled stale food and old cigarette smoke. The plaster walls may have once been white but kitchen grease and nicotine had stained them a sickly yellow. They slid into a booth.

Cal looked around. "No one's here."

Chet tapped the red-painted wooden tabletop with the side of his thumb and glanced toward the back of the kitchen. "Sure there is. Just wait a minute."

There was an eagerness in Chet's voice that made Cal stare at him. After all these years, despite what had happened, the kid was still wide-eyed and trusting. Hell, most of the women Cal knew didn't act that innocent. Chet was even wearing the new snap-button western shirt he'd bought in Butte—as if he were courting some woman, as if she would notice. Why did he need her after all this time? Hadn't he always taken good care of him?

Sunlight spilled through the streaked diner windows like honey.

A woman stuck her head from a doorway near the end of the counter. "Be with you boys in a minute."

Cal saw no more than brown hair flash in and disappear, but he'd heard the voice, the low, throaty tones of a middle-aged woman. He thought about it, trying to match it to the one in his memory—and failing, because he couldn't seem to recall the one in his past. He'd been eight years old when she'd last spoken to them. He remembered she'd said through the wooden door, "Your pa'll be home soon. He'll let you out." He remembered the words but not the voice. He never did figure out why she'd felt the need to lock them up. Maybe she'd been afraid they would follow her, as if they would have gone where they weren't wanted.

He stood and flexed his shoulders.

Chet frowned. "Where you going?"

"I'll be waiting out in the truck."

"Don't now, Cal." His tone was pleading. "She'll be here any minute."

Cal rubbed his hand back and forth across his forehead and finally sat down again. From the corner of his eye, he saw a woman emerge from the kitchen doorway. She grabbed beige earthenware cups from under the counter and brought them to their table. He watched her splash coffee into them without spilling a drop. He hadn't looked at her face yet, but her hands were rough and big-knuckled—scrubwoman hands.

She set the pot on a nearby table, grabbed two menus stuck between the ketchup bottle and the salt-and-pepper shakers, and handed them over. "Be back in a minute."

He glared at Chet. "I ain't stayin' any longer than it takes to eat two eggs."

She was back in less than a minute. "What can I get you boys?"

Chet stared at the menu. "Uh, I'm not sure."

"Well, no rush." One red, chapped hand tucked the order pad into the pocket of her green-and-white uniform. "If you like flapjacks, Harold makes the best around. Take your time. I'll be back."

"No," Cal said. "I've already decided and I can order for him too."

He watched the hands pull out the order pad and hold the point of a pencil against it. He lifted his head and looked directly at her, directly into those weary eyes. She seemed only vaguely familiar. Her faded hair was parted in the middle and pinned back so that it covered her ears in loose clumps. She had dark purplish smudges under her eyes and hollows beneath her high cheekbones. She wasn't a pretty woman, and he tried to remember if she ever had been.

"Two eggs over easy and bacon for me and flapjacks for him," he said, seeing his youngest brother Mel for a moment in the woman's features.

Chet smiled at her. "Please."

She scribbled down the order, then glanced at the cook stove on the other side of the long counter. "Harold'll be back anytime now."

Harold, a squat, broad-faced man with a bald head, came lumbering in and positioned himself behind the grill.

He grinned at them, showing a gap where one of his eyeteeth had been.

"Had to take a piss," he said, then set about firing up the grill.

The woman brought water glasses and silverware and arranged them on the table.

"I thought you might recognize us," Chet said in his over-eager tone.

Cal almost kicked him under the table. He'd said he wasn't going to tell her. He'd said he just wanted to see what she looked like.

She glanced at Chet, then said breezily. "Well, I don't think so. I figured you boys was just passin' through." She poured water into Cal's glass. "You don't live around here, do you?"

"No," Chet said, "but we used to."

She was staring at Cal now, focusing directly on him and growing a little pale.

He turned his head away and took a drink of water.

"What are your names?" Her voice was low and soft.

"This here's Cal and I'm Chet."

"Oh, God," she whispered. She backed up a step and folded her arms across her middle, a hand clutching each wrist.

Cal set his cup down with a smack, so that coffee sloshed onto the table, and fixed his eyes on her. He wanted to see what a woman who could lock her own sons in a closet and leave town would look like when she saw them again.

She pulled out a rag and wiped up the spilled coffee.

Chet was babbling something about leaving today, about having spent a few days in town and seeing Mel, about Mel telling them where she worked. She stared at Chet as though she'd never seen a twenty-one-year-old man before. To Cal's disgust, he was acting like he was sixteen.

She didn't move, didn't even seem to breathe.

"The Navy wouldn't take Cal," Chet said, "'cause he was colorblind. But you probably knew that—about him being colorblind, I mean. They wouldn't take him because he couldn't read the signal flags, which are a lot of different colors. He figured he'd just wait until he got drafted into the Army."

Cal wanted to belt the kid.

Chet grinned. "But the Army didn't draft him, so he went back out to Idaho and we met up there and—"

His voice droned on and on, like a mosquito buzzing or the bacon sizzling on the grill. Between the sun pouring in and the cook stove throwing off heat, he was sweating. The smells of bacon and eggs finally drowned out the diner's stale food and cigarette odors, but they sickened him. He looked around. The joint didn't even have a fan.

Chet was beaming. "We're heading out to Washington State. We heard we can get jobs there cutting Christmas trees. I don't suppose you've done much traveling, but it sure is purty out there."

She hadn't said much, just nodded and murmured, "Oh," occasionally, while looking out of the corner of her eye at Cal.

Harold banged his metal spatula against the grill and yelled, "Order up!"

She jumped as if she weren't used to hearing that a hundred times a day. She walked to the counter, grabbed the two plates and returned with them.

Cal stared at the breakfast she'd set in front of him. "I ordered eggs over easy, not sunny side up."

She flushed. "Oh, I'm sorry." She snatched away the plate and hustled toward the grill.

"Why'd you do that?" Chet whispered.

"It wasn't what I ordered."

"I seen you eat 'em like that lots of times. You didn't have to do that."

She returned shortly and set a fresh plate with eggs

over easy, bacon and toast in front of Cal.

Standing by the table, she said in a soft, tentative voice, "I'm glad to see you looking so good," which launched Chet into part two of their recent history. She scrubbed at the worn tabletop with the rag, absentmindedly, as though she hadn't already wiped up the coffee. Cal thought about how he used to tell the other kids in school she was dead. A few years ago, he'd taken a chance and told the truth to a woman he was dating. He couldn't stand the way she looked at him, the pity on her face, or the shame he felt.

Two farmers wearing bib overalls entered the diner, the door banging loudly behind them. They sat two booths away.

"Hey, Ruth," one of them called. "Where's the coffee?"

She glanced at them. "Be there in a minute." She turned to Cal and Chet and murmured, "Enjoy your breakfasts."

Cal thought she sounded like any waitress in any two-bit diner.

She started to walk away, then turned back. "There's no charge."

Chet dove into his flapjacks.

Cal ate two bites of his eggs. They tasted like sawdust. He looked over his shoulder and watched her take the farmers' orders. Two more men entered the diner, the door banging again. She hurried toward them.

Chet was jabbering about how nice she was and how glad she seemed to be to see them.

Cal splashed salt across his eggs, stared at the saltshaker a moment, then upturned it and drizzled out a white band, three quarters of a circle on the table.

"What are you doing?" Chet mumbled, his mouth full. "You're making a mess."

"It's a C—for us. It means Chet and Cal were here.

I lost my pocketknife. Lend me yours, and I'll carve a C."

"Shit, no. Why would you want to do that?"

He set the saltshaker down and pulled the ashtray toward him. He shook out a Lucky Strike, tamped it on the tabletop and lit it.

Chet shoveled in a hunk of pancake. "The food's not bad."

"I ain't hungry."

He stretched out his legs, leaned back and took several deep drags on the cigarette. Watching the woman scurry around the diner, he felt another kind of shame. Why did she have to work in this dump? He hunched over the table, picked up his paper napkin and held the edges against the cigarette's red tip. Tiny ashes fell.

Chet reached across and knocked the paper away. "Dammit, Cal, stop it."

He dropped the napkin on the table and stood. "Let's go."

Chet looked up at him. "I ain't done eating."

"Let's go," he said, his tone sharper. He fished out a few coins and dropped them onto the table.

Chet wiped his mouth off with the napkin and stood. "She said we didn't have to pay."

"She's a little late."

He was halfway to the door when he realized Chet wasn't right behind him. He turned and saw him by the counter, his hand on her shoulder.

He caught up with Cal, and they walked to the truck.

"What did you say to her?"

"I said we'd stop in the next time we came to town."

Cal tossed him the truck keys. "You drive for a while so I can rest."

"All right." Chet opened the driver's door and climbed in. "She was really glad we stopped by. Made me feel good."

As the truck wove through the parking lot, Cal looked at the windows of the diner. She was standing there, her big hands clutching the coffeepot, tears rivering down her face.

He leaned his head against the frame of the truck cab and closed his eyes. "I didn't feel a thing."

Calling the Roll

In the last four weeks I've been sending messages
to friends and family and colleagues in New York City.
I make a list of each one as if I'm taking attendance in class.
I want to hear each one reply,
"Here" or "Present" or "Yo" or "Hey."
Jessica, Kimiko, Norman, Wendy, Barbara.
Each one tells me a story that begins with where they were
and ends with the word dust and ash.

The children I know were in school.
I want to hear them—Emily and Esther and Paloma—
tell me about their day in school.
The teachers I know were in class.
They've been calling the roll.
Some of their students were absent on that day, but have turned up.
They didn't come to class because they were working,
or sick, or overslept, or didn't finish their paper.
Those were all acceptable excuses, my colleagues tell me.
Some of the poets and artists I know were away from home
on airplanes, in temples, on stage, in residence, in rehearsal.
They all know someone who is in mourning.

In the Buddhist world grieving ends at ninety days.
I don't know if that's possible or that our voices might stop
using words like *tragedy, loss, mourning* and *despair.*
Can we turn away?

A friend in Hawai'i doesn't want to hear another pundit,
or politician, or military strategist use the word *resolve*.
She knows the word doesn't make her feel safe.
I think about my own teacher who told me
that writing was about belief.
I want my students to know this belief,
to say the word belief.

I think about my students and where they are in the world.
Are they calling the roll as I am?
We were in Rome last summer standing
in the footprint of ruins, in ancient Etruscan tombs,
wondering aloud about the lives
of those who were buried there.
I ask my students to consider the spirituality
and symbolism of stairs
as we watch the faithful climb the twenty-eight wooden stairs
of the Scala Santa on their knees.
I follow my students up Borromini's oval staircase
in one palazzo.
Marcia and Nicole and Emily and Joe.
I am continually counting them as we travel.
Is everyone here? Is everyone accounted for before we leave?
Ken and Jessica and Breona and Dan.
Some are out of sight, but I know where they are.

I take them to an island where we feel safe and protected.
We swim in the phosphorescent blue waters of the bay,
our limbs and hands and feet touching each other for assurance.
It is said that there is a hidden ancient pathway
from the water up the mountain.
Instead, we turn from searching for the path
to the sunlight and the open waters.
Sean and Jackie and Becca and April.

Later, after they've left Rome,
They tell me about walking alone at night in Italy,
in Morocco,in Ireland, in Spain, in France,
in Turkey, in Israel, in India.
They stand on the Hill of Tara, in the ancient tombs
of Knowth and Newgrange,
in Rodin's garden, in a Jerusalem marketplace,
in the San Sebastian surf,
on the slopes of Mount Blanc.
They want to be on the ancient ground
of other generations, other civilizations.

They recite what they learned about belief and faith.
Kim and Sandra and Justin and Mansi.
They compare the light in Rome with the light in Spain.
They come home with new language.
They tell me that they've been to places I've been to before,
Places where their fathers had been to before.
Anzio Beach, Prague, Dresden, Paris.

I'm calling the roll now as my students come home
As if they're still seated before me on the stairs
of an ancient amphitheater in Ostia Antica.
I'm counting them for the third time
in case I've missed someone.
They tell me that they haven't been counted
like that since they were children.

—Shawn Wong

LEAVING YESLER

Peter Bacho

This excerpt is from "Leaving Yesler", a coming-of-age novel set in the 1960s in the Yesler Terrace Housing Project in Seattle. The protagonist is an artistic and sensitive young boy who must overcome poverty, answer questions of identity and navigate a perilous adolescence without his protector, a street-tough older brother killed in Vietnam.

Chapter One

BOBBY THOUGHT THAT after his mother died a year ago, things couldn't have gotten worse—but they did. For the last two months, he'd been wandering in a fog after getting news that Paulie wasn't coming back from Vietnam.

Today was no different. He had skipped his afternoon classes at Garfield High in Seattle and caught a bus downtown. On First Avenue, he toured the pawn shops, then the adult book stores—making sure to lower the brim of his dark blue baseball cap to look older and more mysterious than seventeen. He fooled enough clerks to last most of the afternoon, before a bug-eyed, cranky graybeard—probably the owner—told him to buy something, or get the hell out.

Bobby shrugged. He glanced at his watch—twenty to five, close to the time Dad expected him home. Just as well, he figured, as he walked out of the store without saying a word.

On his way home, he walked by a tavern Paulie had taken him to before he went overseas. Paulie, two years older by a day, was in uniform when he and Bobby walked into the joint. Paulie lowered his voice and told a burly bartender with US Navy tattoos on his forearms that this was his last night stateside, and that even though he wasn't twenty-one, he was old enough to die for his country. The least his ungrateful fellow Americans could do was to serve him a Bud in a frosted mug in this, his indifferent hometown. Preferably on the house, he added with a wink.

"And don't forget my buddy here," Paulie said, pointing to his brother. "He's leavin' next week."

Bobby just watched as Paulie's latest Oscar caliber performance summoned a patriotic parade of beers—all on the house. Same, too, with the cheeseburgers and fries that followed.

"Land of the free," Paulie whispered to his brother.

That was Paulie, who seemed to have been born with a swagger—and the physical skills to back it up. Try as he might, Bobby could never quite match his brother's blood—chilling stare and quick fists.

But the differences didn't end there. Built-like-a-beer keg Paulie was dark, just like Dad, and he had oversized knuckles on his thick hands.

Despite being younger, Bobby was slightly taller—and much thinner. But the trait that caught neighbors' attention was the color of his skin. He was much lighter than Paulie, which was hard to figure since Dad was the color of aged mahogany and Mom was part black.

"High yella," many of the kids in their housing project called him, usually behind his back, but sometimes to his face. The black boys would sometimes call him out over that, and he'd always show up, whether he wanted to or not. He had his share of scuffles—but he managed to avoid many more battles because his would-be predators knew full well they'd have Paulie to deal with later.

That's what Cortez had to learn the hard way two years before. Cortez—first name or last, no one knew—was a juvy hall veteran who conked his hair like the other thugs and declared himself to be an up-and-coming gangster, the baddest young brother in Yesler Terrace or any other project. One day, he snuck up on Bobby, called out his name and sucker punched him when he turned around.

As he slumped to the sidewalk, Bobby could hear laughter from more than one source. "High yella punk," Cortez snorted as he and his pals fished through Bobby's pockets for loose change. Bobby struggled to rise, but couldn't because Cortez had placed a size-ten high-top Converse squarely on the side of his neck.

"Little boy, if I was you, I'd stay right where you are," Cortez snarled before turning to walk away.

It took Paulie a couple of days to catch up with his brother's attacker, but when he did he wanted to make sure Cortez would always remember their meeting. A friend told him where Cortez lived. Paulie also found out that Cortez and his buddies sometimes hung out at a convenience store a block east of the Terrace. For at least a couple of hours, they'd cluster near the store entrance, talk loud, drink port from paper cups and use the pay phone to buy and sell drugs.

According to his source, Cortez always began his Friday nights like this. He and his friends would eventually leave—between eight and nine—but would often stop by Cortez' apartment before disappearing into the night. Paulie smiled. That meant they'd be walking up one of the narrow, dimly lit paths that honeycombed the projects.

On such a path one Friday night Paulie jumped out from the shadows and used a 28-ounce Louisville Slugger saved from his Little League days to break Cortez' left shoulder and one of his legs. Paulie chose the ultra-light bat because he knew there was a chance he'd have to slug more than one target. But Cortez' too-high friends, upon hearing their leader scream, fled in different directions, leaving Cortez crumpled on the ground to face his fate.

"That's for Bobby, remember his name," Paulie said evenly, as he turned to walk away. "And if you call the cops, or come after him, brotha man, I know where you live."

The girls, though, found Bobby handsome. More than a few said he was *pretty*—a description that bestowed on its bearer a mixed blessing on the street. Angie, a Filipino-Indian girl who lived two units down, told him he looked like Smokey—as in Smokey Robinson—and *ooh, baby, baby*, her folks were at work so could he please come over and croon to her falsetto words of love?

He declined the invitation—and several others—because how he looked bothered him and led him to questions he didn't want to ask.

Mom said Paulie's looks and attitude reminded her of Dad before the war. Bobby once summoned the nerve to ask her who he reminded her of.

She smiled and kissed his cheek. "An artist, baby," she said.

Mom was right. Bobby loved to sketch and, money permitting, paint pictures of scenes not seen in the projects. But that meant being soft—or worse, being seen as being soft—and in Yesler Terrace, that was a hard ticket to ride, Paulie's intervention notwithstanding. His brother would have shown him how to navigate the shoals of insults and challenges—and fear.

But two weeks short of his return date, Paulie got nailed by a mortar. He wasn't being heroic, or anything like that. He was a draftee, not someone born in red-white-and-blue swaddling clothes, and all he wanted to do was go home, get the military behind him, learn a trade and leave the projects. Going to college and getting a deferment were out of the question. He didn't have the grades, the money, the inclination. He felt the same about catching a bus and heading for Canada. It was too cold there, and he didn't want to learn *Canadian*.

"Hey, man," he once told a draft-eligible friend who was considering the move. "They speak French there, or somethin'."

Besides, an Army tour wasn't forever—or at least that's what Paulie said. "It's like doin' time in juvy," he told Bobby.

A month before he died, Paulie had written and assured the family he'd almost beaten the rap, that he was down to counting the days and hours left and looking for excuses to stay out of the jungle.

"The Viet Cong," he wrote, "will have to find me to kill me." And that's exactly what the enemy did.

Paulie got himself assigned to guarding an air base and was sleeping when the mortar with his name on it ended his life—and ruined the life of his younger brother who was depending on him.

Losing Mom had been hard. But everyone knew the cancer that was chewing her stomach would eventually eat all of it. So when this vibrant, strong woman finally passed, at least a few of Bobby's tears were tears of relief.

But for Bobby, Paulie's death made daily life almost impossible. Paulie would have known what to do; he'd have known what to do with Dad.

Bobby loved his father, but over the last few years, Dad began losing what little he had to start with. First came the dead-of-night screams a few years back, then the daytime lapses where Dad would stare blankly at Bobby or Paulie or Mom—and squint his eyes, as if squinting would somehow repair a broken link in his chain of memory.

Mom told her sons the head blows from a brief, pro boxing career didn't help. Neither did the metal fragments Army docs pulled out of his neck and the base of his skull after a firefight on the island of Samar during World War II. The injuries got him a ticket home, where he rejoined Mom, whom he'd married before going overseas.

"But he's a good man," she said, after the screams and the memory gaps began. "We just need to understand, be patient and love him more."

On the surface and for most of the time, Dad seemed fine, no different from the Filipino fathers of the other old-time Seattle families Bobby and Paulie knew. And other than the docs at the VA, Mom said there was no good reason to let anyone else know otherwise.

As Bobby turned east on Yesler, the shortest route home, his mind wandered to when he and Paulie were children and running unattended up and down this same street. Sometimes, he and Paulie would ambush passing cars with dirt bombs lobbed from behind garbage cans and fences. They'd then duck and listen for screeching brakes—their sign to run. Once, after sunset, Paulie even nailed a police officer who had made the mistake of cruising by on a hot August evening with his window rolled down.

On Saturday nights, Dad's cronies would come visit for a night of poker and booze. The men—Uncle this or Manong that—would sit at the small kitchen table, hunched over and cursing in Filipino as they stared at their cards until the black and white Indian-head sign appeared on the screen of the small television on the counter.

No matter how late they played, Sundays were always the same. Rain or shine, Dad, Mom and the boys would rise early and dress in their Sunday best. But their destination was never St. James, the Catholic cathedral just six blocks away. Instead, they would walk the other way toward Chinatown, less than a mile from their home. Dad would hand Mom a twenty and send her and the kids to eat—and he would eventually join them—but not before spending time with the other nattily dressed old Filipino men clustered near the entrances of different restaurants, bars or dingy bachelor hotels many of them still called home.

Bobby smiled. Great times, he thought, as he turned left on Eighth—the last short stretch before home. But that was two deaths ago.

Since then, Dad had turned inward, losing himself down a tunnel of sorrow and selective recollection. Bobby often had to remind him to cash his disability checks and a small monthly pension from some long-ago job. His father, who used to cook and clean the apartment, had stopped doing either task. Bobby now did both, and often had to serve Dad his breakfast and dinner in bed.

Bobby stopped under a street lamp and raised his watch to the light: five on the nose. Home was just a block away, and if he hustled, he could coax yesterday's bland chicken with enough crushed garlic, vinegar, grease and soy sauce into becoming a reasonably passable meal. Bobby took his cooking seriously, at first because he had to. Now, it was equal parts a matter of pride, imagination and art. He figured he did it pretty well most of the time.

Bobby stepped back into the dark and turned toward home, distracted by the challenge of turning a lifeless chunk of overcooked poultry into something edible. That was a mistake, one Paulie never would have made.

"Be alert and suspicious," Paulie always told him. "Especially here at night."

Bobby ignored that basic lesson of life-in-the-projects wisdom as he walked, head down, wondering about the right balance between soy and vinegar. A matter of taste, he concluded, with his leaning toward a spoonful more of the latter.

That was his last cogent thought. For Bobby, the next

few minutes passed as a blur, with him suddenly on his hands and knees and wondering how he got there, what he should do next. He felt the thud of two quick kicks to his ribs, the second one strong enough to lift him and send him sprawling face first to the concrete.

"Sissy, high yella punk," he heard his assailant grunt. "Too bad 'bout your brother."

The voice was familiar, but far more familiar was another voice—a man's voice cursing loudly, drawing nearer. Bobby was relieved and surprised—and couldn't decide which reaction was stronger.

"Boy, stand still so I can cut you up like, uh," the second voice commanded with a heavy accent. The speaker was stammering, struggling to finish the threat.

"Uh, like a chicken and eat you tonight, yeah, uh, like a chicken," he finally said, sounding pleased.

As painful as it was to move, Bobby glanced up to see the streetlight shimmer off a stainless steel blade thrusting forward and withdrawing, thrusting forward and withdrawing.

"Cool now, old man, just be cool," the attacker said nervously over the sounds of a slow shuffled retreat that quickly assumed a much quicker cadence. Bobby knew he was safe now. His assailant was running, but the new sounds were odd, uneven, like he was favoring one leg over another.

"*Pilay*," the second voice said sadly in Filipino. "Even for a cripple, he's still too fast for me."

Bobby then felt himself being lifted to his feet and having his arm draped around a thick, compact shoulder.

"Saw it from the window, but couldn't get here in time," his rescuer said. "All of this, uh, reminds me."

"What's that?" Bobby asked.

"Gotta keep it together long enough to teach you, boy."

"What?"

"How to duck, son."

Chapter Two

"YOU'RE LUCKY," the emergency room doc told Bobby as he patched him up. He had a couple of broken ribs—but no organ damage—and he'd eventually heal, just don't move around too much.

"Don' worry," Dad told the doctor. "He won'."

For the next three weeks, Dad was true to his word. He resumed cooking—or trying to—but would sometimes find himself standing over a steaming pot and staring at the wall or at the ceiling trying to remember what ingredients to use. When Dad got it right, the stew or the marinated pork, was good to the last bite, just like when Paulie and Mom were still alive. Even when he missed something major—like the liver in liver and onions—Bobby covered it with fresh steamed rice and gobbled it down without complaint.

"Oh, forgot the liver," Dad said on that occasion.

Bobby shrugged. "Still pretty good."

Bobby knew without being told that his father, who was no good with words—at least English words—was trying his best. He was showing his affection through other ways, like cooking. And Bobby showed his appreciation by eating whatever he served.

Dad also called Garfield and told the principal his boy wasn't coming to school this week or ever again, and please save the value of education speech because Bobby wasn't going to do like Paulie and sit through vocational ed classes crammed full of black and brown throwaway kids. Before Paulie's draft notice came, Mom and Dad begged him to try to get into college, any college, but he just shrugged.

"Ain't ready," he said. "It ain't like Garfield ever taught me nothin'."

"One boy's enough," Dad screamed, pleased he was able to make his point without stammering. "Bobby's no grease monkey, he's more'n that."

Dad's plan was for Bobby to go to the nearby

community college—like he and his wife had discussed—where he could finish up high school, pass his GED, start taking art classes, get ready for a four-year school and stay out of the Army. Especially stay out of the Army. Dad figured the war would be over by the time Bobby graduated.

"He, uh, deserves better than what you gave Paulie," Dad said, before slamming down the receiver.

The commotion awakened Bobby, who stumbled bleary-eyed into the living room and onto an old divan. He remembered when Mom and Dad brought it home, courtesy of one of Dad's rare good days at the horse track. But that was years ago, when it smelled brand new and gleamed with a distinctive multi-hued luster, since reduced to must, rusted springs and a run-on reddish brown color. Like the coffee table and the other old furniture in the living room, the divan hadn't been moved from its original spot for years.

Eyebrows arched, Bobby watched as Dad mumbled and paced, seemingly oblivious to his son's presence.

"Dad?" Bobby said softly.

"No way, uh, no way," his father mumbled.

"No way what?" Bobby asked, the tone of his voice still cautious. The old man was obviously upset, and that worried him. If it didn't hurt so much to move, he would have risen from the divan and start pacing himself.

"You ain't goin' back," he said.

"To where?"

"Garfield, told the principal, Mr., uh, well, you know, whassisname."

"But Dad, this is my last year and…"

"You goin' to college," his father said.

Surprised, Bobby couldn't help but laugh. The notion of him in college seemed absurd, like maybe during the next few years he should also consider becoming the King of England. "But you know, college ain't for me," Bobby managed to say. "Or for any other kid from here for that matter, and besides, it costs money and…"

"Me and your mom we saved some money, so you goin' to college," his father declared in a tone meant to end discussion. "Simple as that."

For Bobby, it just wasn't as simple as that. Over the next few days, he tried getting used to the idea, never once voicing his fears to his father.

College? One afternoon, when he was alone, he closed his eyes and tried imagining himself sitting in class, surrounded by students who knew what they wanted. A few months back, he'd heard from the friend of a cousin that the professors expected students to read books and show up for class. The memory dampened his palms. At Garfield, he might do one or the other, but seldom both within the same twenty-four hour cycle.

It wasn't because he was dumb or undisciplined. Unlike Paulie, who'd never met a teacher he could stand, Bobby liked school—at least for awhile. That's why his folks paid the extra money for him to attend St. James. The nuns used to rave about Bobby's imagination and eagerness to learn; they claimed he had a future. But that was long ago.

His Catholic school sojourn came abruptly to an end when one of Dad's late-night dreams became the main feature of an early matinee.

At the time, Dad was working at a fish cannery on the waterfront. One afternoon, he suddenly stopped slicing off fish heads and tails. Knife still in hand, his father approached each of his fellow workers and politely whispered be quiet, please, because the Japanese were lurking close by. He'd seen first-hand how they could turn into snakes and slither through the night to strangle young GIs in their dreams.

That bit of advice got him a red-light ride to the Harborview shrinks, who uniformly agreed any job involving knives and moving machinery should best be done by someone else.

Dad's sudden unemployment meant Bobby's next stop would be Washington Junior High, which drew kids from the projects and rejects citywide who, as a chorus, pronounced it to be the best place in the city to get high or drunk—and not get busted. Washington graduates went to Garfield, but no further. The school's teachers had no illusions or expectations. Most were burned-out public school vets, content to serve their last days in purgatory before retirement. They freely dipped into sick days and, when in class, yawned through the motions as they heard themselves talk.

Their students responded with vacant stares or the unbroken drone of in-class conversations. Each side knew the game—an opening level of indifference matched and raised—everyone killing time until time to go home.

Washington's where Bobby first learned to hate school— or at least ignore half-hearted efforts to educate him. He came to quickly understand the school's main function—as the school district's warehouse for kids with no future.

Now, his father was asking him to rekindle a curiosity he'd allowed to go numb. Dad said the next quarter was starting in a month or so and that when his ribs were less sore, he could catch the bus to the college and register.

"Still got time," Dad said. "Give you the money then."

Dad's willingness to put money on his education bothered Bobby. It was his father's act of faith—one Bobby wasn't sure he had. Arms folded across his chest, Bobby stared out the living room window. On the tiny kitchen table was a pile of texts, undisturbed since he put them there during the first week of his last quarter at Garfield.

Can't promise nothing to his father or himself, he told himself as he slowly approached the table. But lately, he'd started wondering about the subjects he'd ignored. He obviously had time, and now might be as good a time as any to find out.

Chapter Three

A TRIO OF LOUD, rhythmic thumps—paused then repeated time and again—jarred Bobby's bed and awakened him. He bolted straight up and looked out the window, worried the Housing Authority was demolishing his family's rundown apartment without telling Dad or him.

Couldn't be, he told himself. The noise was coming from the living room. As he left his bed and began walking toward the sounds, he realized he was breathing and moving pain free. Surprised, and more than a little pleased, he stopped and gingerly brushed his ribs with his right index finger—a little tender, but that was all. Relieved, he opened the door to see an old canvas heavy bag—its innards kept together by rolls of electrical tape—swinging from the beam of the walkway joining the kitchen and the living room.

"No place else to put it," his father explained between grunts of three-punch exertion. "A little crowded, sure, but this gonna hafta do."

Mouth open, Bobby watched his father as he'd never seen him before. Bathed in sweat, he seemed also to sweat off some of his almost sixty years as he moved slowly around the bag—space permitting—then stopped and fired right jab, left cross, right hook combinations that shook his target. Dad kept this up until an alarm clock buzzed and stopped his left cross in mid-flight.

"Tha's it," Dad declared, as he took off his bag gloves and rested, hands on knees, gulping down air. "Enough for today."

"Dad?"

"I told Antonio to get my stuff outta storage and bring it here," his father explained, as if what he said answered any question Bobby might ask. "So tha's what he did this morning."

Dad often stumbled into the gap between idea and expression, at least when using English. Bobby needed clarification. "Huh?" he asked.

Antonio, or Uncle Tony to Bobby, was one of Dad's long-time pals who still lived in Chinatown. According to Dad, he and Tony boxed together on West Coast undercards before the war, and that Tony returned to the ring for a few paydays after he left the Army.

Tony had tried to persuade Dad to join him—"Like, you know, old times in 'Frisco, Stockton, places like that," Tony said excitedly—but Mom put her foot down. "'Ceptin' I won't be here when you come home," she said.

Dad's wartime wounds hadn't healed, she said. Monkey see, don't mean the other monkey gotta do. Simple as that. Besides, he was too old. In fact, he and that fool Tony both were. And besides, she hated the sport—if it could be called that. Just to be sure, she made Dad get rid of his new sparring gloves, shoes and all of his other gear, in case he got weak and changed his mind.

That's how Dad's old equipment, now scattered about the living room, ended up in Uncle Tony's storage locker, unseen by Bobby until this morning. Now the gloves were back, freshly oiled and shining. Same, too, with his father's boxing shoes that had the sheen—if not the scent—of new black leather.

But it was one item in particular that caught Bobby's eye—an elegant black satin robe with red and white trim laid carefully across the divan. Bobby walked over and felt the smooth, cool fabric.

With his fingers, he traced the longhand name embroidered on the back—"Paulito 'Kid' Williams"—and felt for a moment the depth of his father's twin passions.

"You took Mom's name?" Bobby asked, still staring at the robe like it had once been worn by Jesus or some top-of-the-line Catholic saint.

"Yes," Dad answered. "Wanna try it on?"

Surprised, Bobby glanced at his father, then turned away. "No," he said slowly. "It's yours, you earned it. You try it on."

Dad smiled. "Okay," he said, as he lovingly donned the robe. He smoothed out the clumps and carefully inspected the length of each sleeve before striking a pose—hands raised, right fist forward.

"Still fit," Dad declared triumphantly.

"And Mom made you give up boxing?"

"She asked me to," he answered softly. "Simple as that."

Bobby didn't believe him for a moment. He knew the decision must have been a tough one—and admired his father even more for making the choice. But why did he choose now to show him this part of his past?

"Oh, I still got work to do," Dad explained with a shrug.

"Do what?"

"Show you the basics," Dad answered. He paused for a moment before speaking again, like he was carefully weighing the impact each word might have on his son. "Uh, like uh, how to duck," he finally said.

According to Dad, ducking was one skill he didn't do especially well—and he'd paid a price beyond the scar tissue lumps over both eyes.

"Neuro, uh, neuro," Dad stammered, searching for the rest of the word.

"Neurological?" Bobby asked, remembering Mom's reference to his father's condition.

"Yeah, yeah," he giggled. "Tha's it, the docs say I'm damaged that way, but not all cuckoo, jus' a little, uh, I think."

"Geeze, Dad, I didn't even notice," Bobby lied.

His father smiled, unsure he believed him. "You're a good boy," he finally said.

"No, really, I mean…"

"Whatever," his father said, interrupting Bobby's attempted

explanation. "Now, hold up your left hand, put your left foot forward. Your right hand, hold it back by your cheek."

These instructions were barked—clear, concise, a rarity from his father—and Bobby did, or tried to do, as he was told. Dad started walking around his boy—tucking an elbow here, extending or drawing back a fist there. He then took two steps back—like an artist examining his latest creation—and decided, nope, not there yet.

"Your chin," Dad barked.

"Huh?"

"Tuck it in," his father said, followed by a pause, further examination.

"This how I'm gonna fight?"

"Nope," Dad said, as he continued his inspection. "Keep holdin' your hands up."

"Then why…"

"Cuz most guys'r right handed and this is how most guys gonna fight you."

"But…"

"To beat those guys and to stay safe, you gotta think like they think, know how they throw it, when they throw it, what they gonna bring," Dad explained.

What Dad said made sense, but Bobby's motionless pose was getting harder to hold by the moment. His lead left hand started dropping, same, too, with his right.

"Dad."

"Keep 'em up," his father commanded without looking up. He was trying to figure out the right balance, how much weight Bobby should put on each foot, how deeply he should bend his knees.

"A little lower, the left knee," he said. "But keep keepin' 'em up."

Bobby sighed, but did as he was told. "Thought I was gonna learn how to duck?" he said, trying hard not to whine.

"You are," Dad answered calmly.

Chapter Four

ACCORDING TO DAD, Bobby shouldn't worry too much about an opponent's left hand.

"Tha's just to jab you and distract you, then nail you with the right cross when you're lookin' where you shouldn't be," he explained. "Tha's the t'under that puts you on the ground."

The right hand, he explained, was usually the knockout hand. That's why fighters held it back so that when they saw an opening, it could move over a longer distance and gather speed and power.

According to his father, the answer was to turn around and fight southpaw—with the right hand and foot forward—and to keep circling right and away from the t'under. Dad explained that boxing was about patience and cunning, about finding the best angles for attacking and defending, not just about throwing punches. The best fighters usually find a way to hit someone, without getting hit in return—and that was something the southpaws he knew were pretty good at. That's how he fought, and for the most part, it worked pretty well, except when he'd lose his temper, abandon what he was supposed to do and just march straight in and brawl.

"Too hot headed to be a good southpaw," he explained. "A southpaw's thinkin' all the time and I'm thinkin' you're a smart boy, smarter than Paulie—he was more like me. So mebbe it work good for you."

Dad smiled and walked up to his son. He took Bobby's left hand and stretched it so his two big knuckles touched the bridge of his nose.

"Here, I'll show you," Dad said. "Try and hit me with your jab and right hand. One two, fast as you can."

"But Dad," Bobby protested. "I don't got no gloves."

His father shrugged. "So, who wears gloves in a streetfight?"

"But…"

"Right here," Dad said firmly, pointing to his forehead. "Throw."

No choice in the matter, his tone said. But just as Bobby flicked his left, his father—who, a moment before, had been standing in front of him—slipped under the punch and stepped outside his arm in a smooth, seamless motion. At the same time, he threw his left shoulder into a belt-level blow. Bobby felt the knuckles of Dad's left hand pop his belly and stop. Another blow—delivered, he assumed, by the right hand—hooked his kidney hard enough to let him know both punches could have been much harder.

Bobby grunted. Helpless, his right hand still guarding the side of his chin, Bobby looked over his left shoulder to see Dad standing to his side.

Hands up, his father was focused and leaning every-so-slightly forward. He seemed to stare through Bobby, eager to attack again.

"Dad," Bobby said nervously.

The sound of Bobby's voice turned off a dangerous switch in the old man's brain. He blinked his eyes and slowly lowered his guard. He was relaxed now and smiling, not recalling the details or direction of the short-circuited stroll he'd just completed.

"See what I mean, Bobby?" he said casually. "Hard to beat you do it right."

"Yeah, yeah," he replied between deep breaths. "I see what you mean."

YOU NEVER CAN TELL
IF THE WATER IS TOO DEEP

Stella Cameron

When pride, confidence and trust are almost fatally wounded, the battle to be whole is tough.   After losing everything, Annie Duhon has made it back to a life filled with hope—and the danger that can come with wanting acceptance too much.

ANNIE DUHON had forgotten how to dream. Or forgotten how to get started on a dream, maybe.   A fluttering in her belly felt familiar—and it didn't feel bad. How long was it since she'd last known she didn't feel bad? If the fluttering wasn't a dream (she did have a sort of fantasy sensation where she saw colors in her head) it could be something to do with hope. Whatever it was, she'd take it.

The bayou was low and she sat on the bleached knee of a worn-down cypress tree. Scummy pea-green water had retreated enough to leave the stump all but dry at the base and from there she studied the way water hyacinth spread over the gently heaving surface. Annie had lived in Louisiana all her life, in St. Martinsville, St. Martin's Parish precisely, and her mama said they hadn't had such a long dry patch since Annie was a skinny little girl.

Didn't feel natural.

Most things didn't feel natural.

Sure was hot enough. Her cotton dress stuck to the skin on her back and sweat drizzled down the sides of her face. She jumped at the sound of a splash and watched a fat, white nutria pulling its thick-tailed body out of the water. Time was when she would have tried her hand at catching the tasty rat for dinner. Her mother made the best nutria pie in the parish.

Today she wanted to look decent more than she wanted to see her mother smile and if that was mean, then so be it. Time came when a girl had to look out for her own needs.

Maybe he wouldn't come after all.

Until three weeks ago, Annie hadn't had a plain old date since the third year in high school when she got pregnant and had to find a job. She didn't like to think about all that. Her little girl's lungs hadn't been properly developed when she was born and they couldn't keep her alive.

That was then, ten years ago, and this was now. She wanted to start over. All because of a pair of kind eyes looking at her over froth on the top of a beer glass, and the way a man put the glass down so slowly, never glancing away, Annie Duhon thought she might be coming alive again. He was to meet her here today. At first she wouldn't believe he actually knew *her* before she'd seen him at Petunia's Gumbo in town. But he did. Martin Samuel reminded her how they'd glanced at one another in a library in Lafayette six months earlier.

Hoo mama, how a little thing could change your life. Annie took classes at the junior college, traveled there three evenings a week because she was going to make something of herself. She had her GED, but now she needed real qualifications to work her way up from boxing cakes at a local factory. She wanted to be a cook. People looked up to a good cook and Annie just knew she'd always have a desirable job if she could run a kitchen. Could be one day she'd have her own place—something like Pappy's Dance Hall down by Toussaint.

Annie's Dance Hall. Best eats and best music around.

In that library she'd sat across from Martin. Just once. When he mentioned the occasion, she recalled seeing him and thinking he was one of the nicest looking men she'd ever seen. But they hadn't met again until three weeks ago. Martin said he'd been looking for her. How he had found her, she couldn't guess. They'd had four dates and today would be the fifth. Why not ask him how he had been clever enough to search her out?

Clouds slid over the sun and the trees threw darker shadows on the water. Faint skeins of shading cast by mossy beards hovered between reflected branches.

"You givin' up on me, Annie Duhon?"

She smiled and looked at him over her shoulder. "What makes you think you've been on my mind at all?" Warmth gave her a little giddy feeling, warmth from being happy.

"Oh, don't you be coy with me, young lady. What you doin' here, sittin' on that stump, if you aren't waitin' for me?" He walked toward her and showed no sign of concern at the damp ground pushing up around his shoes. "Answer me that, girl. And remember, tell the truth and shame the devil."

Annie laughed. He was one of those tall, rangy Cajun men. Black hair, black eyes, olive skin and too appealing to be healthy—for a woman concentrating on getting to be a real good cook and changing her life.

He drew close, bent over and put his big hands on his knees. "I do believe this is the best view I've ever had of you," he said, not smiling anymore. "You're a lovely woman,

Annie, with the nicest smile I ever did see. Everythin' else about you is nice, too."

Annie felt her cheeks get red. She turned her head away from him and remembered her mother's warning. *Don't you ever forget how a sweet talkin' boy got you pregnant and cost you more than any girl should have to pay. This time it's a man and the only difference between a boy and a man is a man is bigger, stronger and slicker. Men and boys want the same thing, it's all in how they go about gettin' it.*

The heat in her face throbbed. That had been before her last date with Martin. This time Mama didn't know where Annie was or what she was doing.

"What is it?" Martin touched her arm. "Have I offended you? Come on too strong? If I have, I apologize and I'll be more careful in future."

"You were nice," she told him and jumped from the cypress knee to stand on the soggy dirt. Finding him so close surprised her but she stayed right where she was. "I've had some busy years trying to make a life for myself and I'm out of practice with pretty talk."

He offered her a hand and she held it. Well they'd met five times now and he'd shown no sign of trying the kind of things Mama feared he would. Why shouldn't she hold his hand?

"I brought us a picnic," Martin told her. "After a bit I'll run back to my car and get it."

"Lunch time's gone," she told him quietly, smiling up into his face.

"But dinner isn't," he said. "I thought we'd wander over to a little spot I know and talk awhile. When the sun goes down a bit more and we're hungry, why, then we'll eat."

They strolled along the edge of the bayou before Martin led Annie up a little rise where a faint path showed, to a rotted-out wooden bench in front of a willow tree. He sat on the bench and indicated for Annie to join him.

Gingerly, she perched on the silvered slats. "It'd be a shame to spoil this bench by fallin' through it," she said, and giggled. Gradually she wiggled her way to lean against the back. "Well, I'll be. Would you look at that. You can still see the water from here. I thought it would be hidden."

"Not hidden," he said. "An inlet curves around there and comes this way. Did you tell your mama you were meetin' me today?"

"No, not this time. Why?" She hadn't wanted another lecture.

He put an arm along the back of the seat behind her. She didn't mind. "The other day I thought you didn't seem yourself. You were edgy."

"I was fine." She most certainly had been edgy.

"Annie"—he turned so he could see her face and pulled up a knee—"I would like to meet your mama."

"Why?" That was an inappropriate response but he had shocked her.

"Because you and I aren't children. We know somethin' special's happenin' with us and it's happenin' fast. Don't you think your family should be included?"

"We've only met five times," she said quietly. "Six if you count the library."

"Exactly, and I think about you all the time." He shook his head. "Forgive me. I'm goin' too fast for you but this never happened to me before. I haven't known many women because I always figured I was lookin' for one special one. Now I've found her I want us to share our happiness with those who care about us. Next weekend I hope you'll let me take you to meet my folks in New Orleans."

Annie's heart thudded so hard it hurt. "I see."

Martin was quiet awhile.

"I like sitting here with you," she told him.

"But you didn't understand what I said to you—about feelin' somethin' special between us?"

Annie messed with a thread hanging from a button on

his shirt. "I do understand." She leaned closer and wound the loose piece around and around beneath the button so it wouldn't fall off.

"Do you feel the way I do, *cher*? Would you hate it if I asked you to marry me?"

Her head buzzed and she thought she must have misheard him. Things like this didn't happen to Annie Duhon the loser. Now, she shouldn't put herself down like that. The nice people who helped her get well after.... She'd made mistakes in the years after her little girl died, but those people at the rehabilitation place taught her how to respect herself again.

She looked at Martin and he smiled at her. With his free hand he gathered up both of hers and held them against his chest.

"I like you a lot," she said.

"Enough to marry me?"

He wasn't making fun of her after all. "Well," she said, tentative. "Yes, I like you enough for that."

"Poo yi!" He let his head hang back and he laughed. Then he hugged her to him. "I was scared to ask but I'd made up my mind I would. Once I make up my mind I don't change it. You have made me a happy man."

Annie's pulse flattened and she couldn't get quite enough air.

"Do you like this?" Martin kept on holding her but reached into a pocket. With Annie in the crook of his arm, he showed her a ring. "Would you do me the honor of letting me put it on your finger?"

"It's beautiful," Annie said of a dark ruby in an antique gold setting. She held out her hand and he slipped it on her finger. "I don't think I should take it," she told him. "You don't really know me."

"I know you as well as I need to. That was my grandmother's ring. She gave it to me for the woman who becomes my wife. That's you, Annie."

What would her mother say? She would like Martin, how could she help it?

The ring looked elegant on her long-fingered hand. She started to giggle, couldn't help it. She and Martin were engaged to be married. They'd never as much as kissed. He treated her with so much respect, just like you'd expect a gentleman to do.

They both faced the bayou but Martin pulled her close. "I don't want to wait," he said. "We don't need to go through all the ritual. Talk to your mother and see how dates work out for her—we'll do it together. Three weeks should be all we need to get ready."

Annie's heart got tighter. Her life was going to change. She'd known it would, but not so soon.

He stroked the side of her face. "Would you like to give up your job and go to school full-time? You know I travel. I want you to do whatever makes you happiest so you'll be busy while I'm gone."

School full-time. Annie covered her face and let her hair fall forward.

"Hey, hey, *cher.*" Martin rubbed her shoulders and neck and kept his fingers there beneath her hair. "You wouldn't be cryin', would you?"

She shook her head. Tears ran down her cheeks but she laughed and hiccupped.

"I have rushed you," Martin said.

"No, no, no. I'm so happy."

Annie looked into his face.

He wiped the tears from her cheeks.

She wanted him to kiss her and brought her mouth closer to his.

Martin put a finger on her lips and touched his own to her brow. "I sure do want you, Annie."

He wanted her. A man like him who could have any woman he wanted. He must expect her to say something but she couldn't think what. *Please don't let him get mad.*

"Listen to this place," he said, his voice gentle. "Some would think it silent, but everythin's talkin'."

Annie's stomach quit hurting. "I like it here," she said. Waving willow branches swished and cast shadows over Martin's face. Small animals skittered in the brush, crickets clacked and she even heard faint creaking in the cypress trees and the sound of Spanish Moss catching against peeling bark on the trunks.

"It's noisy," she said, smiling at him.

A pirogue swayed through the water, a man standing at the oar and two small children sitting one behind the other in the middle of the narrow wooden boat. The children screeched with laughter.

"It's hard to find a little peace that lasts," Martin said, sounding annoyed. "Let's go, it's time for our picnic. I don't like an orange sun. Looks like it's bleedin' to death."

The orange sun he spoke of lowered in the sky, sending fiery shafts through the trees and lightening the color of the water. Annie thought it beautiful. "We should eat," she said. "I'll help you bring the food from the car."

"It's gettin' cold," he said, although Annie hadn't cooled off one bit. "We might eat in the car but that isn't what I had in mind. Maybe we could go to your house and eat. We could wait for your mama. We need to talk."

"Mama won't be back till late. She's with her sister."

At first his silence worried her. He was working out how they would do things. Men didn't like it if you messed with their plans.

"You're right," she said. "It's comfortable at my house and we could wait for Mama to come home."

She could see he liked the house. It was a single story, surrounded by trees, and Annie and her mama kept bright potted flowers along the gallery.

"It's nice out here," Martin said. He parked his car facing the narrow lane leading from a rough road to the Duhon place. "Secluded. You and your mama made a good choice."

"My folks bought it. Dad died two years ago and left the place paid for so we get along fine."

Martin got out and came around to help her from the car. He ruffled her hair and said, "We're going to need a house of our own—in New Orleans. Your mama won't like that but she'll feel better when we tell her she can be with us whenever she pleases."

They climbed to the gallery and Annie let them into the house. "The kitchen's at the back and the window's so close to the trees we can pretend we're picnickin' after all," she said. It felt funny to be in the house with Martin— alone. Not that she didn't know she could trust him.

"I want to tell you somethin'," he said suddenly. "I should have made sure you knew everything about me before I asked you to marry me."

He walked past her, straight to the kitchen and leaned against the sink with his arms crossed.

"Don't look so unhappy," she said. "We all have things in our past we wish we could forget."

"You couldn't have anything bad in your background. You're untouched. Annie, I was married before but my ex-wife wasn't a good woman. I had to divorce her."

Of course he'd had a life before they met. So had she. "I'm sorry," she said. "You wouldn't have done it if you hadn't had a good reason. I had a baby, Martin. When I was in high school. She died and I still feel sad about it."

"Thank you," Martin said. "Thank you for believing in me enough to tell me that. We're going to be so close, *cher*. Annie, come here and let me hold you."

He met her in the middle of the kitchen and they clung together.

"We've made a commitment," he said.

Annie whispered, "Yes. I never expected to have this much joy."

"This is just the beginning. Purgin' the soul takes time. Annie, I'm exhausted. I didn't get much sleep last night and it's been the kind of day that wrings you out. Maybe I should go. Your mother won't appreciate a man who's fallin' asleep while he talks."

A panicky feeling shook Annie. "I don't want you to leave me. Not now."

"And I don't want to leave you—ever—but I need to be sensible."

"Take a nap till Mama gets home. She'll be another couple of hours. Sleep here."

He shook his head. "That wouldn't look good."

"Oh." Her face felt hot. "Why, it'll look just fine. You can sleep in my room and I'll bake something for after dinner."

"You're tempting me."

She smiled. "Good. Oh my, how long is it since you ate? We never had our picnic."

"I'm not hungry now but I will be later, in time for your bakin'."

"Come on, sleepy boy," she said, leading the way to her room at the front of the house, across from the tiny sitting room. She opened the door and walked in ahead of him. "Don't laugh at the frilly stuff. Mama likes it and I think she pretends I'm still her little girl."

Martin came behind her and put an arm around her neck. "It's okay for her to think of you that way. Innocence is easy to love." He kissed her ear, ran his tongue around the inside. "It's so easy to love you. I shouldn't ask, but would you lie with me? I need to feel your warmth."

She struggled to find her voice. "I shouldn't."

"No, of course not. Forgive me. I'll go now."

"You'll stretch out on that bed. I'll hold you till you sleep."

Martin picked her up and dropped her on the bed. He sat beside her, held her wrists above her head and kissed her. Annie could scarcely catch her breath. She'd never been kissed like that before. His tongue reached into her throat and flicked back and forth. When he raised his head his face had flushed, and his black eyes shone bright. "You're so beautiful," he said. "I bet you're beautiful all over."

He excited her. Inside, she trembled.

"Can I do the things I want to do? We are goin' to be married."

Annie stared up at him and drew in a sharp breath when he sat astride her hips. He released her hands, slid the straps of her dress from her shoulders and pulled the bodice down to her waist. She didn't wear a bra. Panic bubbled into her throat. She watched the top of his head, the glimmer on his dark hair when he licked her breasts, bit her nipples. "This isn't right," she told him, not wanting him to stop.

His response was to pull her arms free of the straps. Once more he took her hands over her head but this time he produced lengths of twine and tied first one, then the other wrist to the rails of the wrought iron bed. Her finger stung when he wrenched off the ruby ring.

Annie tried to fight him, she struggled, but his body pressed down on her and she was no match for his strength.

"I want to stop," she said clearly. "Please let me go, now." Be firm, she'd been told. Don't do anything you don't feel comfortable about.

"That's not what you said to the boy who fucked you in high school. Or to the men who paid your rent and kept you in drugs in New Orleans for years."

She couldn't speak, couldn't think. Why would he behave like this? Why would he put a ring on her finger and talk of marriage, then do this? How did he know about her shameful past after the baby died? Annie started to cry.

"Shut up." He pushed her skirt up to her waist and tore off her panties.

"Don't," Annie said. "I'm not a bad person, not anymore. If you think I am, why did you want me?"

He laughed. "When you went down in the woods today, you shouldn't have gone alone," he sang. "Those people in the pirogue spoiled everything. No one comes up that inlet. I should know, I've studied it. Everything would have been perfect. You were going to drown and no one would ever figure out how. This is so much messier." He pinched her belly hard and laughed when she cried out. Pitching his voice higher, he said, "Mama won't be back till late."

Annie shook so badly her teeth clattered together. "I'm not sure when she's coming home. I knew there was time for you to nap and feel better is all."

"You're terrified," he said. "I like to see a woman terrified. I like her to struggle and wish she'd never met me. Women like you wouldn't get punished without men like me. A woman like you made me HIV."

The panic roared out of control. Annie screamed, and Martin slammed a hand over her mouth before he ripped her bodice apart and crammed fabric into her mouth. She gagged. He caught hold of her hair and turned her head to one side. "Oh, no," he said. "No choking to death till I'm ready, tramp. Once a tramp, always a tramp."

Blood pummeled her eardrums. The orange sun had died and shadows filled the room, turned it black and white in her eyes.

She felt him tie one of her feet to the bed and kicked at him. He finished and grabbed her flailing ankle. With her legs splayed wide apart, he secured the second foot and immediately stuffed her cotton panties between her thighs. He pushed them into her while she choked and cried.

"There," he said, still at last. "You lie there and think about the things you hookers do to decent men."

From his pants pocket he took an old lighter. He eased it apart and dripped stinging fluid between her legs. With the lighter back together, he flicked a flame to life.

Annie's eyes filmed over. When she wailed her pain, the cloth in her mouth moved deeper into her throat. She smelled burning hair, felt scorching skin.

From somewhere close she heard her mama call, "Annie, whose car is that outside? Who is with you? I've brought someone you used to know. He's been lookin' for you. You're gonna be surprised."

Martin turned toward the door, his features stretched wide, tight. He started in that direction, then returned to wrench the twine from one of her wrists, smother the dying flame.

"Lyin' bitch," he muttered. "Filthy, lyin' whore."

And a man shouted, "Somethin's burnin'. In that room. Call the fire truck."

Mama had come home early. She and a stranger would come in here.

Staring about, his eyes wide and glassy, Martin spun around and rushed the other way, banged into the foot of the bed as he went.

He ripped back the lacy curtains.

Martin couldn't get the window open.

GREATEST HERO EVER

Jim Molnar

What was it Elwood P. Dowd said in "Harvey"?
"Nobody ever brings anything small into a bar."
Elwood, of course, brought his 6-foot, 3-inch rabbit.
In "Greatest Hero Ever", make room for even bigger things like
dolphins and Alaska and God, love and hope and honesty.
Still, some small things linger in the lounge, too,
around lonesome bar stools and in
conversations across ingenuous tabletops

IN THE LOUNGE, at the bar, he sat nursing a beer and rolling crooked butts from a crushed yellow pouch of Top, with matching papers. The guy had been drinking and smoking for quite a while, and philosophizing with the barmaid, who told him he reminded her of some country singer whose name she couldn't remember. "Same hair, same mouth, same beard," she said.

"There's only one thing that scares me," he said in a resonant voice that lent an evangelical authority to his words. "Pygmies. Why, you ask? 'Cause they're cannibals down there in Africa. Pygmy cannibals."

"You ever been?" the barmaid asked, glancing down to the far end of the bar in hope of spotting something to wipe at a polite dislocation. "You ever gonna go there, to Africa? And they aren't about to come here, so what's to worry about?"

"Just knowin' there's cannibals out there, that's enough," he said. "Knowing stuff is important. Education. You know the best way to get an education? One book. Read just one book. Open the dictionary and read it. A college education right there. It's all you need."

The man's blue work shirt was wrinkled, open over a red and white T-shirt almost to his soft belly. His jeans were clean and generously tented in seat and thighs. A Caterpillar baseball cap was stained with sweat and oil from his fingers, with which he regularly tugged at the brim. The beard, the country singer's beard, was ash gray with a faint memory of red.

He spotted me sitting alone at a corner table with a book.

"Nice quiet place—comfortable," he called from the bar, waiting for me to raise my head and offer the invitation of eye contact.

I nodded. "Nice," I said. "Good place to read."

"Yup, nice and comfortable and peaceful. Almost perfect." He stood from the bar stool. "There's only one thing …"

Cannibals.

"… one thing. If only there was one person who'd walk in here right now …"

"Really? Any particular person? Or just someone?"

"I wish she'd walk in here right now," he said. "Myra. We could talk." In the silence he seemed to hear her voice. The memory of her closed his eyes. "But I'd have to be honest with her. I would. I love my ex-wife, still love her more than any other person. Except maybe my parents. But more than any other, other person I ever knew. She told me to get out, you know. It was because I was too honest. Myra couldn't take too much honesty. Some. She could handle some honesty up to a point. Only not too much. She wanted someone less honest than me. But if she walked in here right now we could talk ..."

"Think she—Myra—think she could handle honesty any better now?" I asked.

"I wouldn't know," he said. "Mind if I sit with you? But I'm kinda already with you even over here. Small place. Nice. Comfortable. One thing it could use though."

"Myra?"

"A radio. Good music. Tuned to KLBS."

"Ah, the oldies station, good music."

"But there was a better one before that. A better station. KYT. You know that one? I'm Tom Terrific." He walked over to the table to shake hands. "Tom Terrific," he said. "I'm Tom Terrific." He held my hand, looked into my eyes, awaiting recognition. "Dude and Dude. Morning show."

"Tom Terrific," I said. "Wait a second. I should have guessed with that voice of yours. Tom Terrific the DJ."

"That's me," he said, grinning, pumping my hand. "Tom Terrific. With Dude. We were Dude and Dude. 'It's a good morning here in Ukiah. Time for music and good humor with the Lords of Laugh.' "

"Well, well, Tom Terrific. So, you still on?"

"Left it. After a while, y'know, you want to see people, look into their eyes when you're talking with them. Got bored, I guess you could say. Not a bad job. Work four hours a day. Then the other four you go out and meet the public, shake some hands, cut some ribbons, do some promotion. But it got boring."

"So what are you doing now?"

"Food service. Famous Food Service. On the phone. Seventh biggest remote shopping service in the Western states. 'Hey, I'm Tom Terrific, the radio guy, and I'm just calling to ask if I can have a few minutes of your time to talk about good food. Wouldn't a big juicy steak taste good right about now?' Telemarketing. I'm pretty good at it. Very good, actually. I could make Famous Foods the third best in the West. Why not?" He sat down.

"So you like it."

"I told them I needed honesty."

"Honesty?"

"I walked into the office yesterday afternoon and I said, 'You know what you got here? You got Tom Terrific. The best. But I'm not gonna build this company without a little honesty. You choose. You want, you need honesty.' That's what I told 'em."

"Tom, aren't we talking telemarketing here? What's honesty got to do with it."

Tom Terrific bristled. He tugged off his cap, wiped his hand back across the thin dun-ish curls plastered to the crown of his head, then pulled the brim back low to his frown like an aging pitcher holding a full count. He peeled a tissue out of the Top pack, unfolded the pouch and poured a thin line of tobacco. Rolled and licked, the cigarette was oddly angular at one end, pinched to a point at the other— a recreational-style roll. He struck a match from a wilted book that advertised mail-order diplomas. The empty paper at the tip of the cigarette caught fire and flared, carbonized and collapsed back to the first shreds of tobacco which extinguished the flame in a billow of acrid smoke.

"You got nothing without honesty," Tom Terrific said, wincing through the smoke. "They use me and my name and my reputation—hey, I'm Tom Terrific, see?—and I got a right to protect that with the truth and nothing but the truth."

"What's the issue? What do they want you to say?"

"Mahi-mahi."

"Mahi-mahi?"

"Yeah, familiar with it? Right. So they tell me, 'Tom,

just say it's shark. Somebody asks, just say it's shark.' "

"But it's not shark."

"I know that. That's what I'm talking about. I looked it up, you know. In the dictionary. There's a lot of knowledge in there. A college education right there—just read that one book and it's all you need. The *Third Collegiate*. That's the one I've been reading. The *Fourth* just arrived at my house a couple of days ago. It's in both of them, mahi-mahi. I checked. Anybody could do the same. I could say mahi-mahi is shark and they could walk over and pick up a dictionary and check it out, and you know what they'd find?"

"Well, they'd …"

"They'd find out just what I found out. Dolphin. Mahi-mahi is dolphin for godsakes. Dolphins breath air through holes on their backs for godsakes. Big brains. Pointy noses. Those cute little smiles. Flipper. 'Say it's shark,' they told me. But they're selling Flipper for people to eat."

Tom Terrific used his two big hands, soft like a clerk's but gritty, mucky under the fingernails like a laborer's, to push himself back from the table and out of the chair. "If you'll excuse me for a moment, I have to go."

The barmaid walked over as soon as he stepped around the corner to the men's room. "He bothering you? I could ask him to leave, no problem," she said. "I mean if he's bothering you or anything. He's not exactly a regular here, y'know."

"No bother," I said. "He's OK. Just needs to talk."

"He's a talker, all right. Don't get him started on pygmies or cannibals. He's got a nice voice, though."

"He's Tom Terrific," I said. "Used to be on the radio?"

"Don't I know it. Got that story a couple of hours ago. And a few times since." She shrugged, retrieved his half-finished pint of bitter from the bar and set it on the table with a fresh coaster. "Just signal me if you change your mind. Pygmy cannibals. Dang. Used to be Communists, then Arab terrorists. A little knowledge is a dangerous thing, as they say."

"Pygmies aren't cannibals, by the way," I said.

"That makes me feel better. You gonna tell him?"

"Nope," I said.

"Right. He'd probably only start worrying about something else. Might as well worry about something you don't need to worry about."

Tom Terrific sat back at the table and took a sip of beer. He picked up the coaster and turned it over. "Hold on," he said and walked over to the bar and asked the barmaid for his old coaster.

"You want the truth?" he said, holding it up to me. "Here's the only truth you have to know. Simple as 1-2-3."

"Guinness?" I asked.

"On the other side here," he said. He turned the coaster over. "What's it say? Read the word, man."

Tom Terrific had printed the letter, all capitals, and surrounded them with a sunburst of lines, a halo of hash marks. He'd added embellishments at the four main compass points, arrow points and a crossbar:

GODISNOWHERE

"So, what's it say?" he asked, narrowing his eyes to the challenging stare of an Inquisitor. This was a test.

"God is nowhere," I said slowly, realizing immediately that I'd given the wrong answer. "God-is-no-where," I repeated, more slowly; then, triumphantly: "God is now here. That's it, right? God is now here."

"I can see you're a man of thought and perception," he said. "No more needs to be said." Tom Terrific seemed slightly disappointed that I'd solved his puzzle and had obviated the need for instruction. "It's a pleasure to meet you. A pleasure to sit across the table from a good and honest man. You can see honesty in a person's eyes, you know. I see it in yours. I look for it in mine every time I look into a mirror. I want to make sure I'd like myself if I met me in a bar. An honest man."

"Well, thank you, Tom," I said. "That's quite a compliment."

"You know where you can find people—a place that kind of breeds them naturally? Alaska. That's the place. I'm kind of from there myself, once removed. But I like to think of myself as being from there. Alaska. My great-uncle built cabins there, in Moose Pass, way up in the Kenai Peninsula. You been there?"

"Been to Alaska, but only to Southeast. Sitka, Ketchikan…"

"I hadn't actually been there, myself, to Alaska, until a couple of years ago. Just heard the stories, you know, and saw videos on cable. Then a buddy of mine couldn't use his ticket and he gave it to me to take a cruise. You been on a cruise?"

"On a big cruise ship? No, I …"

"Man, you ought to go. Never seen anything like it, sailing up the coast from Vancouver—the forest, the glaciers, the islands, whales. Ketchikan, Skagway, Juneau—in Juneau I just stayed on the boat. Never did get up to Moose Pass. But Glacier Bay. Oh, man. I was standin' out there on deck and heard this sound, like thunder—thought it was thunder, actually. The glacier calving, you know. Pulled out my video camera but didn't get to turn it on until it was all over. But I still look at that video and remember what it was like. The video just shows these blue hunks of ice floating there, but I remember what it was like, what happened just before. Oh, man. Most magnificent thing I've ever seen in my life. Took this float plane, too, over the Juneau ice fields. Magnificent. If there was any question in your mind, it'd be gone after that." He held up the coaster again, like a priest raising the consecrated host at Mass. "God is now here."

"See any bears or anything?"

"I could have taken one of those shore trips, but, hell, I guess I can live without bears. Ain't that the truth, though? Anyone stand a better chance of living if he doesn't get too close to a bear."

Tom Terrific chuckled, slicked his hand through his hair and pulled the cap back into place.

"So this is my idea," he said. "Building a Web site, a Tom Terrific Web site, and putting stuff about Alaska on it. Some of the pictures I took, descriptions of it all. Just so people will know about it. Get people to go and experience it. I'd be like the evangelist of Alaska. Did I tell you, my great-uncle built cabins up in Moose Pass?"

"You did."

"There's that part of Alaska in me. I could feel it when I was there, pretty close to there, anyway. In the trees, the glaciers, the stars. You'll never see stars like that anywhere else, at least I haven't. You have to stay up real late, like three o'clock in the morning if you're there in summer, to see the stars like that, because of the midnight sun, you know. But, man, the Big Dipper, the Little Dipper. I looked it up, you know, in the dictionary. It has other names. It comes from the Greek, the other name for it. I don't remember the Greek, but I remember the translation. Charles's Wane. That's another name for the Little Dipper. Imagine that. Seeing it up there now, I think, 'Tommy's Wane.' Charles's Wane, but me, I think of it as Tommy's Wane."

"You're in the stars, Tom."

"I remember when I looked it up. 'Dipper.' It was pretty close to the word 'disestablishmentarianism.' That's a heck of a word."

"I had an aunt by that name," I said.

"What's that?"

"Took her forever to write her signature."

"Yeah? Well, I sign my name Tom Terrific most of the time. That's who I am, you know. My given name is Thomas Francis Kornbluth. But I've thought of myself as Tom Terrific for so long, that's who I am. When I was a kid, there was this cartoon show I loved. It was about a little boy who wore this crazy funnel for a hat, and there was Mighty Manfred the Wonder Dog and the bad guy, Crabby Appleton. Anyway the boy had curly blond hair like I had, and—oh, man—he had powers, like he could change himself into anything he wanted."

He sat up straight, tilted his head back and sang, drumming the table and whistling his own accompaniment: "'TEE-RIF-FIC! I'm Tom Terrific, greatest hero ever. Terrific is the name for me, 'cause I'm so clever. I can be what I want to be and, if you'd like to see, follow, come follow me. If you see a plane on high, a diesel train go roaring by, a bumble bee or a tree—THAT'S ME! When there's trouble, I'm there on the double. From Atlantic to Pacific, they know TOM TERRIFIC!'

"And that's who I am."

Tom Terrific rolled another cigarette and readjusted his cap.

"Honesty is what I stand for," he said.

"Tom, tell you what. When you get home, check the dictionary again," I said. "It could help you out at work maybe."

"What do you mean?"

"Well," I said, "first of all, why do think the people at Famous Foods want you to tell customers that mahi-mahi is shark?"

"They didn't explain it exactly," Tom Terrific said. "But I think they figure that people'd like the idea of eating Jaws but not Flipper. Flipper, for godsakes. I mean, I don't want to eat Flipper. I wouldn't eat Flipper. Sure, in the beginning, God told us we could eat anything. He told

Adam that. Maybe it was Noah. He told somebody though. But still, it's like cannibalism. If we can eat anything, I guess God wouldn't mind even if we ate other people, like the Pygmies in Africa. If it was a matter of life and death, God would probably shrug his shoulders and say, 'Go ahead. When you gotta, you gotta.' But mahi-mahi isn't a matter of life and death, y'know. Heck, I still watch that show on the Nickelodeon channel. Flipper. I love that channel."

"But, Tom, if you look up dolphin again ..."

"I mean, Catholics, right? Catholics believe they eat Jesus on Sundays. Like the Iroquois eating the still-beating hearts of their enemies to gain their powers and their virtues. Who was that priest, that missionary? Mon Pere ... Somebody. Joliet. Wore this big black sombrero; had this expression his face, saintly but scared and angry all at the same time as he was holding the cross out in front of him like a lantern. Like a divining rod. Divining rod—hah! Get it? I loved that story when I was a kid. Loved the pictures. Him going down the river in that big French canoe until the Iroquois caught him and ate his heart out."

"Tom, if you look up the word, though, I'll bet you'll find out that there are two animals that are called dolphin. One, the bottle-nose kind like Flipper, is a mammal. It's a cetacean, a small toothed whale; it breathes air."

"Right, through a hole in its back. That's what it says."

"But I'll bet if you look again, you'd see a another definition, a second one. There's another animal, a fish, like any other fish—a game fish—that's called a dolphin, too."

I turned over another coaster and tried to draw the outlines of the two dolphins, one with the familiar beak and smile and flat flukes like a whale; the other with a more angular, flattened head and gills and a vertical tail like other fish. "Something like that," I said.

"Hold on a second," Tom Terrific said and called to

the barmaid: "You still have that dictionary back there behind the bar, sweetheart?" He grinned. "That's what I mean about this place. How many bars you know that keep a dictionary under the counter?"

The barmaid dropped a raggedy old *Random House* on the table and left quickly.

"This ain't as good as the *Collegiate*, but it's OK." He paged through to dolphin. "And here's 'disestablishmentarianism' again. OK, so let's see ..."

"Check to see if there's a second or third definition for dolphin," I suggested.

"OK, so, here's 'small toothed whale' ..."

"That's the mammal."

"And, two, 'any of a medium-sized game fish' ..."

"That's the one. That's mahi-mahi. This one," I said, pointing to the drawing.

"Says it changes color when it's pulled out of the water. Now that must be pretty."

"But it really is a fish. Not Flipper."

"Maybe that's what they mean when they—they started telling me it was like a tuna or something."

"Maybe," I said, "they just figured it wasn't a good sales pitch if you went into a whole lot of detail, explained the whole thing. Shark, saying shark, is easy."

Tom Terrific closed the dictionary and sat thinking. "Still, it isn't honest."

"In a way, eating shark is just as bad. There are a few shark species that are becoming threatened because people just kill them for sport or cut off their fins to send to Asia for soup, then just leave the rest to die."

"Ain't that something?"

"So, did they fire you? Can you go back to Famous Foods if you want?"

"Well, I kind of left. But I told them I'd give them a day or two to think it over."

"Do you want to go back?"

"I told them, 'I could make Famous Foods third best in the West. I'm Tom Terrific.' That's what I said."

"Maybe," I said. I started packing up my books and drained my coffee mug. I pushed my coaster drawing over to Tom Terrific. "I'll bet you could find a picture of a dolphin like this in the encyclopedia. You could look it up. But I have to get going, really. Maybe I'll see you again in here every once in a while. It's a good place to read."

"Well, I sure liked meeting you. Always looking for an honest man and good conversation. And, y'know, maybe I will. Maybe I will go back and tell them I've thought about it some more, that I found out some stuff."

"That'd be good, Tom," I said. "Terrific."

He tugged on the brim of his baseball cap. "That's right," he said. "But I'm also gonna tell them I expect some honesty. Dolphins aren't sharks, you know."

THE LOYAL ORDER OF BEASTS

Kay Kenyon

*Where do story characters go when the books are closed? And do
they have to live up to what they used to be? Questions like these
are fine fuel for stories in the realm of speculative fiction,
my preferred literary landscape.*

*Paco dreams. In sleep, the boy falls into the kingdom of
enchantment where roam fantastical beasts, gatekeepers, dragons,
and helpful allies. Where escape is always a wish away, as unicorns
leap from their corrals, and maidens rappel from their turrets. And
when a boy meets a hungry dragon, he will figure something out.*

*When Paco wakes, the night visions evaporate like soap bubbles
popping. That is a rule of the Realm. You cannot stand in both
kingdoms at once.*

GRENDEL SHIFTED in his chair, trying to get his old
bones comfortable, waiting for his number to be called,
trying to salvage another bad poker hand. Through magic,
he could conjure a royal flush, but his poker buddies

expected more of him. He was Grendel, monster of legend. A big deal once, and long ago. Did you have to live up to what you used to be? That was always the question for legends.

Most of the guys in the lodge were has-beens, sitting around playing cards instead of off on adventures. Unlike the self-important, inflated egos of the Realm who indulged in tedious replays of their quests—the Loyal Order of Beasts committed itself to good works, bringing a little magic into the Mundane World. In dreams.

Grendel glanced at the mirror on the wall, hoping to see his number appear, but so far, no such luck.

He and his poker buddies, Rudy and Polyphemus, had been lodge members so long they'd worn their chairs into the shape of their butts, a far cry from the glory days of heroism and epic meaning. These days *heroic* was out of favor, corny even. All that mattered to the new breed was box office on the latest movie, toy-store tie-ins, and gross receipts. The fickle mantle of fame. Grendel could tell them how fickle, but who listened anymore?

He glanced at the table in the corner where some of those new characters were playing a high-stakes game of one-eyed jacks. Slouching, cards held close to the chest, they glared at the mirror, sneering at folks whose numbers got called—a sad commentary on the state of lodge civility. This was a *fraternal* order, after all, not a biker bar. Not that it was strictly fraternal anymore, either.

Rudy glanced up at Grendel. "So. You goin' to visit the little kid again?"

"If my number comes up, I am."

Rudy rolled his unlit cigar to the other side of his mouth. "Won't do any good. Kid's autistic."

"That's why he could use a little magic."

Rudy shrugged, allowing Grendel his point. In truth, the World needed the Realm. The Mundane World was bound by all those picky rules of science—rules that left the place pitifully short in the imagination department. So Realmers sneaked it in—into that shared ground of dreams, where it could inspire mere humans. The World created the myths, and the Realm housed the resulting immortals. A neat little feedback loop. The connecting path was the Isthmus, a bridge between worlds, traditionally managed by the Loyal Order of Beasts.

Problem was, the World wasn't creating decent legends anymore. These days the Big Mundane produced mostly those media-types; over-wrought, empty characters that arrived pumped-up with their own hype. They usually took up the fast life, stomping around castles and battle fields, forcing a bunch of yokels to play bit parts to their star power. Who was that one slob from some action movie? Jaba something. Came into the Realm lording it over folks, whining and demanding attention . . . .

Rudy dealt Grendel another lousy card. Polyphemus was staring at his own hand with that single-eyed intensity only a cyclops could muster.

Looking around the room at his fellow beasts, Grendel had a sudden and unwelcome view of how seedy the lodge had become. The folding chairs, the shabby flourescents, the lingering smell of disinfectant soap. It used to be nicer, didn't it? For one thing, they didn't use to let in women. Whoever heard of a female scaring the bejesus out of you? Well, there was Baba Yaga, the Russian witch, living in that creepy house with the chicken legs. You couldn't take a myth like her and foist her off on the women's auxiliary. Besides, women had improved the lodge. Decent food. The number system instead of pitched battles to decide whose turn for dream duty. It was better. Sort of.

At thoughts like these, he felt a familiar weight settle on his chest. The old ticker wasn't what it once was. The apothecary had given Grendel a potion, and he took it faithfully, immortal or not. Having a vial of medicine made him feel proactive. Because, all around him, the world was taking on dark little spots. In his peripheral vision, shadows gathered—but when he looked dead-on—nothing. Disconcerting. What was it they said about not being able to identify a threat? It caused anxiety. Not a problem you'd ever have had in the old days. But it seemed to fit now.

"Gren," Rudy said, raising the ante, "you don't look so good."

"Yeah? And your mother was a troll." Grendel threw down a few coins, staying in the game.

Rudy put on a hurt face. "*I'm* a troll."

"Still."

Rudy tapped his unlit cigar on the table edge, shaking off imaginary ash. Grendel had to admit the hall was better since the women banned smoking, second hand smoke being bad for the heart. Old guys like him had to be careful. Take those smells he was subject to lately, for example. Spore-ridden, bloated smells like tuna sandwiches on the turn. They said weird smells could be a precursor thingy—an aura—before a seizure. Removing the vial from his pocket, he took a little nip.

"Your problem, Gren?" Rudy said, reading his mind, "you worry too much."

Rudy had a point. When had Grendel become such a downbeat? Immortals didn't have to worry about heart attacks and the like. And females in the lodge were nothing to get all bothered about, the way they played bridge, and bet quarters. Kind of sweet.

No, if you wanted a real problem, it was those other guys. The new boys on the block, always lurking at that corner table. Their type was nothing more than slasher-hackers, getting story impact from gore and body counts. You take death, with its implications of sacrifice and transformation, and turn it into a bloodbath. Scary, yes. Uplifting, no. Grendel campaigned against them, but the twinks got their memberships. Rudy argued that the lodge needed new blood, and Polyphemus caved in too, despite the fact that the candidates hadn't even read *The Odyssey*.

Or *Beowulf*, for that matter.

The mirror on the wall lit up with a new number: eighty-one.

"That's me." Grendel folded his cards and pushed back his chair. As he stood, his heart clenched, like it just got an over-friendly handshake. He paused, getting steady.

Rudy waved the cigar at his friend. "Have a good one."

As Grendel passed the table of punks, one of them reached for a new card, knife-hands glinting. The rotten tuna smell was stronger here. These creeps could really use a bath.

Snip snip, came the sound in his wake. One of the morons waved his slasher hands at Grendel's big ass.

No respect.

A silvery downpour ran over Grendel's scales as he entered the enchanted forest. That was strange, since it never rained in the Realm unless it was a trumped-up storm for, say, King Lear, who was so big on reenactments.

In front of the cave entrance, Grendel shook himself, scattering raindrops from his back. Looking around, he was surprised to find the cave unguarded. Bluebeard was usually the gatekeeper on duty. The fellow didn't have much else to do these days, now that it was mythically incorrect to menace young women—and now that those same damsels were as likely to burn his beard as take any crap from him.

Grendel conjured up a note, pinning it to the side of the cave: *What, you guys taking coffee breaks these days? Geez. Grendel.* Stunts like that made the Order look bad. In the old days . . .

Aw, the hell with the old days. He was eager to dream

up a good one for Paco. That was one thing that never changed for the worse: kids—at least the little ones. Paco needed good dreams, if anyone did. Couldn't even recognize his parents' faces. Yeah, dream world was about all that kid had.

He hesitated before plunging into the abysmally dark entrance. Without Bluebeard's chattiness and shrewd pointers on Isthmus conditions, Grendel felt like a trespasser. Also, and annoyingly, he became acutely aware of his heart beating, and the thought occurred that if you paid attention to it, you'd throw it off stride, so to speak, causing little what did they call thems—arrhythmias. He reached in his doublet for the vial and took a swig. Then he strode into the cave.

The Isthmus jumped into being, fanning out before him, about six spans wide, arcing into the smoky void of nowhereland. The bright surface of the bridge was quilted, as though Here must be stitched to There every step of the way.

Grendel could see maybe a hundred yards down the Isthmus. When he got to the limit of his vision, as always, he would see another hundred. What was different these days was how his feet sank into the way-fabric and left impressions, like skin that has lost its elasticity. The Isthmus was growing weaker. And smaller. Every time you touched the sides—if you got tired and staggered, for example— the Isthmus got a little smaller. That's why the lodge needed the numbering system. Only room for a few crossings at a time.

In the glory days, the Realm and the World had freely mixed. He'd heard it said that the worlds began by overlapping, and had been separating ever since. Some expanding universe theory, or such like. These days, the Realms didn't touch, except in dreams. But over the millennia, the Isthmus suffered from too much traffic, such as from hoards of orcs, and swarms of fairies, that sort of thing. All these picky rules for how the Real and the True could mix. Yeah, Real and True. The Mundane World was Real, all right. But the Realm was True, and if you didn't get it the first time you heard it, you never would.

Here before him were the footprints of Baba Yaga, her stiletto-heeled boots making a track like a zipper. It formed a rut, and not springing back, either, like it would have even a few dreams back.

"Grendel?"

He jumped, chest thudding.

A shadow on the side of the road wavered, then snapped into the form of a beefy white guy. He looked familiar.

Grendel staggered against the wall—he hadn't realized he'd strayed so far that way—and jerked his hand back from the forbidden contact.

"That you, Gren?" the man asked.

"Bluebeard?" Grendel approached the fellow. It was him, all right. But no beard. "What the hell happened to you?"

Bluebeard rubbed his chin, perhaps discovering for the first time that he had one. "He challenged me, this guy did. So what could I do, I just played along, you know how folks are about their little myth deals. He says, 'Gatekeeper, I come to slay you,' or some such, and I said, 'Well, have at it, asshole,' expecting the usual mock combat, and then the fucker ripped my beard off." His voice wavered as he patted his unfortunately receding chin. "That wasn't supposed to happen."

"Shit," Grendel said, feeling stupid that he couldn't think of something more empathetic.

"You're telling me?" Bluebeard looked incensed at Grendel's remark. "No skin off your nose if I lose the one thing I ever loved."

"Who was it that did it?"

"That punk. That guy with the mean manicure. We never should of let in somebody that couldn't even do the handshake. You know? And now here he is, taking your role, the stuff *you're* supposed to do."

"Tell me about it. I was against it from the start." Underneath his calm words, Grendel was thinking that nothing like this had ever happened before, and that the dark spots he'd been seeing were massing into a storm.

Meanwhile, Bluebeard was still dealing with his loss. His eyes pleaded with Grendel as he said, "I look just like a beefy white guy."

Grendel shook his head, denying it, though it was horribly true.

"What kind of person would *do* this?"

The words came to Grendel: "Someone who enjoys pain."

Confusion spread over Bluebeard's face. "The pain of personal growth? The pain of the betrayal of human love? What?"

"No. Pain for the sake of pain." Bluebeard was living a fairy tale. And that punk wasn't.

"Son of a bitch." Bluebeard pursued his lips. "I'd better get back to the entrance. I don't even know how I got here, but I'm on duty. None of the rest of those new guys are getting in."

"Good man," Grendel said. "But one thing? I need that book of yours." Despite the beard fracas, the gatekeeper still had the huge tome tucked under his arm. "You wrote down who's gone in, and what their assignments were?"

Bluebeard nodded, handing the book over. "Going after the asshole, huh?"

Grendel looked down the length of the Isthmus, in the direction of the World. "A scary dream is one thing, but the scare has to *mean* something. If these guys are just into nightmares, I'm going to drum 'em out of the Order."

He took a little nip from the vial to steady himself. Brave talk. But now that he'd said it, he had to do it. Unlike in the Real, in the True you always kept your word.

The longer he walked, the madder Grendel got. The Order had been slipping from its high standards for eons. Little lapses, small compromises. Then big ones, like letting in the movie monsters, ending with the nadir of popular taste: slashers and hackers. In that slow decline, you never got your Big Test or Final Battle. It was honor lost in increments. Like the science-types said, entropy prevails. To keep a state of order, effort must be applied. Without work, a hero dissipated into commonality, even in the Realm.

He was forced to admit that this dissipation described himself, too. And, worse, he'd known it, all these years. That ticker problem? It was nothing but his immortal body wincing in disgust.

Sweat dripped from his brow as he stopped to check the book. He was nearing the end of the bridge, and would have to make his insertion accurately. His claw traced down the page, *Laing, Zlotnick, Le Sueur, Castillo, Dowling, Lopez*— this guy had been busy.

Grendel would begin at the top of the list, with Laing. He hazed his vision, altering his focus for that dimensional catapult into the kingdom of dreams. Then he mopped his brow and, filled with the energy that comes from a good dose of indignation, made the jump.

Laing, Laing: looking for a dreaming Laing . . . Through the haze of the dream state, Grendel could see Laing's back porch where the man had been sleeping to escape the South Carolina heat. But there was no dreaming Laing, only a pervasive smell of wrongness. The porch screens held back one hundred and eleven mosquitoes, their feet picking across the mesh in a delicate longing for blood. But the punk had gotten there first.

Laing's fine dark skin had once held this mundane man together—but now all that remained was a red debris and the smell of death. Grendel had to sit down. Sweat pouring, heart swelling like it collected that sweat and could expand no more.

The slasher had moved beyond dreams.

There had been rumors of this new generation of Beasts. Unholy mixtures of magic and science that could actually touch the other realm. He had thought it was all made up. Not everything you could think of came true, thank the gods. But a new, more cynical, era had bred—straight from the human mind—monsters able to slake the new appetites for shock and mayhem. And the Loyal Order of Beasts had them in its *fraternal* embrace.

He staggered to his feet and opened the book again, hands shaking.

Zlotnick, Le Sueur—if the slasher had gone in order, those would be Grendel's next stops. Then his nail traced down to the last name in the registry. *Lopez*.

A shadow fell on Grendel's heart like dew on a cool glass.

Taking your *role*, Bluebeard had said. *The stuff you're supposed to do.* Paco was Grendel's assignment. And his last name was Lopez.

The bridge elongated just then, extending another hundred yards. Grendel plodded on, afraid to run because of his sagging heart, but lugging his huge body along as best he could. His feet hurt under his weight, and as though in response to that thought, the bridge jumped again, adding on yardage. *Knock it off,* Grendel whispered. That old dream stunt, how you kept going and never got anywhere, such a cliché. He needed a good oath to sharpen his purpose, and uttered, *As God is my witness.* Less than inspiring, that old movie line, with Scarlet kneeling in the Georgia mud, spoiled and selfish to the bitter end.

This time with feeling, he whispered, "By all that's True," and dragged his scales and bones down the damn expanding Isthmus.

He didn't have a plan. He didn't know how a Realm monster got Real, and he didn't know how he could save Paco, but nothing was going to get saved if he didn't arrive there in time. The first rule of the heroic quest was to show up.

At last the bridge settled down, and he got within range of Paco's dreaming head. The boy's visions welled up from the other side, making bulges in the Isthmus, marking the insertion point. Tossing the book down to get his hands free, Grendel blurred his vision and jumped. Behind him he left a divot on the way-fabric, a cleft that remembered his leaping hind feet for a very long time.

Paco lay sleeping. As usual, he slept in the little shed in back that he preferred to the company of his five brothers and sisters.

Relief washed over Grendel. The boy, his hair a damp tangle on the pillow, clutched a favorite blanket, sleeping soundly. Grendel could see these details from his position under the boy's bed—a metaphorical position under the bed, from which spot a Realmer could cast up a decent dream by lying on his back and feeding off a youngster's sense that there *was* something under the bed.

But that smell.

For a second Grendel thought he'd trailed it with him from Laing's screened porch.

A noise at the door, where a blanket covered the opening. It was just the faintest skritch of claws on wool, but Grendel knew the slasher had arrived.

Grendel crawled out from under the bed and stood beside Paco, forming a dreamland scrim between the boy and the monster.

The slasher had the face of a human, but knives for hands. "I thought I smelled a wet dog," he said. "Get caught in my diversionary rainstorm?" He squinted to bring the phantom that was Grendel into clearer focus.

"Yes I did. A nice touch, that rainstorm. Foreshadowing

the ugliness to come."

The slasher shook his head in pity. "It's a mistake to think figuratively about real things, Grendel. You're used to chasing metaphors, but it's a poor substitute for experience—you know, the crunch and muck of real life."

"Real death, you mean."

The slasher leaned against the adobe wall, seemingly at ease, perhaps open to reason. "Can't have one without the other. Once you get past your horror of death, you realize that it adds intensity to life, gives it its meaning. Not that I expect you to see."

"Whose death are we talking about, here," Grendel spat out, "this little kid's, or yours?"

The slasher paused. "Well. Bear with me here." He took a few quick steps over to the foot of the bed and peeked at the boy. "Fine, he's still in alpha." He glanced up at Grendel. "I like to give them a premonition before I take them. I signed on for dreams, and I keep my word."

At this reference to the Order, Grendel's outrage swelled.

The slasher continued, "Once I manifest in the World—as now, for example—then I automatically incur death. Here today, gone tomorrow. Much too temporal for my tastes. So, I make up the gap by letting the kid die for me." He frowned. "Is that a metaphor? I was never good in lit class."

"No, it's not a metaphor. It's a crime."

"Nicely said. A good feel for dialogue, Gren. But what is the topic here, exactly? I have work to do."

He reached past Grendel—actually through Grendel—and picked away Paco's blanket to gaze on the boy's bare shins, glowing faintly in the spill of moonlight from a crack in the ceiling. "Kids look so sweet while they're asleep, don't you think?"

While they'd been talking, it occurred to Grendel that this Big Test he was in the middle of might take a sharp turn for the worse. Might, in fact, be fatal. After all, to be heroic, something had to be at stake. Usually something big. His chest filled with a draught of calming air.

Grendel wasn't sure how to manifest himself, so he winged it. Gathering his thoughts, he released the Realm with all his strength. While his heart scrambled like a cat brought too near a swimming pool, he untethered from the Isthmus and fell into the Mundane World—all of him, heavily and finally.

A plume of nausea moved through him, and vanished. He was Real.

The slasher cocked his head. "Bold," he murmured, impressed in spite of himself. "Yes, indeed. But I fear you're not Real material. The boys won't accept you. You're too old, too limited in your thinking." He squinted as though trying to imagine Grendel as a slasher. "Sorry."

Grendel steadied himself, reeling from the transition, but braced by the slap of cool, Real air. "Not your fault if you're a little slow to catch on here," Grendel said. "Perhaps we should step outside where we can talk without waking the kid."

"Lead the way," the slasher said, pointing his knives at the door flap.

"After you," Grendel said.

The fellow took a parting look at Paco. He was making little scissors noises with what passed for his fingers. Snip snip. Then he strode over to the door, ducking past the blanket.

Sage smells and cricket songs lent an earthly charm to the night, but such delights must be short-lived for Grendel.

"Time's a wastin'" the slasher said. "Don't you love these Mundane sayings? Anyway, cough it up, I'm busy tonight."

Here in the World, Grendel towered over the slasher. He could kill the fellow, and he was up to the deed. But on the other hand, he wasn't the Being he once was. The old ticker, once a metaphor for his lack of life purpose, was now in fact a defective heart. He might not stand up to old-style hand-to-hand combat. If he lost, Paco was the sacrifice.

"Take me in his place," Grendel said. "I'm Real now, my death is as good as the boy's." Doubt passed over the slasher's face. "Maybe better. Think of it, the glory of taking Grendel down. It'll add to your mystique—Grendel is still a big literary name."

"That was the St. George deal, right?"

"No, but you've got the general idea. Kill a legend, become one yourself."

But the slasher was shaking his head. "No, you missed a piece here. I like to shed a little blood, sure. But frankly I get off on, you know—the fear."

"Oh, don't worry about that. I'm afraid." Those shivers weren't his scales drying in the hot night breeze.

"Yeah?" The punk came closer, his nostrils flaring.

Grendel's mouth went dry as he smelled death under the slasher's armpits. "Yeah."

Again, the little snip snip noises, as the slasher-hacker came to a decision. "OK, deal."

"Your word is still worth something, even in the Real? You'll leave Paco alone?"

The slasher raised his eyes dramatically to the night sky. "As God is my witness."

Grendel winced. "Could you make another oath than that one? My dignity, I still have a little left."

"Oh." The slasher pursed his lips. "OK, I swear by . . . by the Loyal Order of Beasts."

The final insult. But maybe Bluebeard had been right. The Order had brought this upon itself.

Now the time was come for Grendel to think of a worthy last utterance. In the Realm it would have been a cinch. But here, Grendel had heard, the usual last utterance of a heroic airline pilot about to crash was, shit.

Grendel crouched down, and exposed his neck. "I'm ready." In a way, he'd always been ready.

It must have been that the slasher took pity, or that a moment of decency unaccountably took hold, because when he snapped out his knives, he drew them quickly over Grendel's neck, not lingering, and finally, not mutilating either. But Grendel's blood spilled from his neck in shuddering pulses.

The slasher moved off, toward his next nightmare. He paused at the edge of the courtyard. "Puff? You know, the magic dragon?"

"No," Grendel whispered, "wrong again." The guy was hopelessly illiterate.

Then he was alone, lying in the Lopez back yard, his heart emptying itself in the dirt, forming a shallow red pond. His irrelevant thought was, how was the world going to explain the body of a monster lying here?

He stared up at the night stars, those wondrous natural pearls, thinking how much he would have liked to spend more time in the Real. In one thing, at least, the slasher had been right—about the intensity thing. These last moments were vivid, more than some eons had been in the Realm.

Hearing a noise at his side, he opened his eyes. Paco. The boy wrapped his shirt around Grendel's throat.

Grendel tried to pull away. "No. Leave me be."

But Paco kept on, unafraid of Grendel's monster shape. Paco had laid his blanket atop Grendel like a postage stamp on a hippo.

Helpless before the boy's ministrations, Grendel lay staring at the night sky as the stars left tracks on his vision.

Sometime during that long night he told Paco about his life. He thought the boy would get bored and fall asleep, but instead he sat cross-legged in front of Grendel, and it encouraged the old Beast to talk. He told about his beginnings, the *Beowulf* story, and then about the Realm, and the creatures there, both heroic and craven. He mentioned Rudy and Polyphemus and even the media stars who, in retrospect, seemed more deserving than Grendel had once thought. He told of all the Beasts that had touched his life, those who had risen to the status of myth, and those who merely kept the old stories alive.

Paco brought him water in a dog dish, and Grendel was not too proud to sip from it.

As morning came on, Grendel found that a little strength had returned. He believed that he might have time for one last thing.

"Sorry about all the blood," Grendel told Paco. "You're not afraid, are you? Because monsters aren't going to be bothering you anymore."

Paco watched him with full, round eyes.

"On my honor," Grendel said.

Then he heaved himself up, and testing his legs for a moment, side-stepped into the Realm.

On the Isthmus he noticed how dreadfully he stank. No help for it. He found the book where he had dropped it, and managed to magic up a pencil to write down what had happened—the Final Test of an aging hero, and the last adventure of the Loyal Order of Beasts. Then, winding up, he threw the book with a mighty cast, skittering it along the Isthmus like a flat stone on a pond. He hoped it reached the Realm, but with stories, there was no guarantee of forever.

Then he went to the Isthmus wall nearest him and began beating on it. He hammered with his fists, and when they became too weak, he lay on his back and kicked with his strong back feet, using his mortal body to hammer at the walls that brooked no mixing of the realms. Under the assault, the bridge darkened, and as it did, Grendel's body began sinking into the deep folds. The Isthmus was dying, along with him. Those old dark spots at the corners of his eyes had always been death waiting, in a figurative premonition of what must be. It was sad to think that, as the Isthmus passed away, the Realm, too, would gradually atrophy. He was sweeping it all away, for the sake of all the dreamers who counted on their dreams not to slay them. For the sake of never letting another slasher go over to the World. It was true that now the World had one real bad ass. But he could be killed. It was the price he paid for being Real. Even in the World there were a few heroes who would relish such a task.

With his strength finally spent, Grendel rested, laying his head on the quilted pillow of the bridge.

Then the path that Baba Yaga had tread along the Isthmus opened up like a zipper and let in the dark.

In the Realm, Rudy stood with the Book in his hands, his troll's heart moved, in spite of himself. Polyphemus put a hand on his shoulder, steadying him.

"It wasn't supposed to be like this," Rudy said.

Grendel's words spoke to him from the page: *There are some good things about temporality, Rudy. The stakes, for one thing. They're higher. You got to take a stand. You got a few good years left. Make them count.*

"But what about our poker group?"

Baba Yaga. You need an anchor legend.

Rudy allowed as how that might be true. "But how about the World? How will the Mundane get by without us?"

They'll think of something. They usually do.

Paco lies dreaming. He dreams of unicorns and beasts, half-man, half-monster. He conjures fire-belching dragons and fairy

queens in gossamer carriages, as well as beings never seen in any realm at any time. He remembers tales told at the lake of blood, where a voice had spoken to him all night long, a voice that had often soothed his terrors and painted his imaginings. He dreams some of these beasts, as well as new ones.

And as he dreams, an Isthmus begins to form....

That Shadowy Figure

That shadowy figure at the window
is myself decoding holiday lights
laced across bushes and snaking along
branches into next year. Time is a mask
made of filaments burning to show us
a good time at a distance. These are
the leftovers whose owners designed
themselves for the future. Heaven
will come to Earth or Earth to Paradise.
A succession of neighbors has tried
opera, the Classics and hot tubs seeking
the sublime, and for years a dog whined
all day to be left alone. We are at the center
of this particular spinning wheel, up
early or late to bear witness. There is
an echo within the barred owl's keening,
"Who-cooks-for-you?" An answer turns
our heads, and another, and then the sky
darkens around each star because
of beauty accompanied. She stays awake
with me as the evening shortens,
bedrooms darken and streetlamps dim,
and for those who dream, it begins.

— *Marvin Bell*

GUESS WHO'S COMING TO TOWN!

Meg Chittenden

*When someone who looks a lot like Santa Claus moves in across the
street, Joel is convinced the man is there to spy on him.
This makes him very nervous—deservedly so.*

THE FAMILIAR, roly-poly figure wore a red outfit
trimmed with white fur. And glasses. Little round wire-
framed glasses. He appeared behind Joel's closed eyelids
early one morning while Joel was resting in that tranquil,
half-dormant state that occurs between sleeping and
waking.

The man in red was more of a flat, cardboard
representation than a three-dimensional person. From his
merry cherry of a mouth, which was surrounded by a
generous amount of white whiskers, a cartoon balloon
issued forth, each word in it bordered by pulsating light.

"GUESS WHO'S COMING TO TOWN!"

Joel chuckled as he swung his legs over the side of the bed. Why the hell was he dreaming about Santa Claus in the middle of the hottest March he could remember? Why not the Easter Bunny—right now there were chocolate eggs, plastic grass and stuffed rabbits in every store window.

He had become clairvoyant, he decided the following Saturday. That's when he first saw the man who had just moved in across the street. It was hot. Joel was wearing shorts and a tank top while he mowed his front lawn. The lawn didn't actually *need* mowing, it hadn't started in on its spring growth yet. But Sahara Brown, the pulchritudinous young neighbor who had rented the house to the right of Joel a couple of months ago, was lying out in her bikini on her chaise longue and he wanted her to see the muscular results of the iron pumping he'd been doing since Marian left him.

This surprised him. He had been so upset when Marian left him he'd thought it might be years before he ever showed interest in a woman again. Once bitten and all that.

Sahara was something to behold, from her delicate pink toenails to the top of her wildly curling hair. A man's hands could get trapped in all that hair.

Neighborhood gossip had it that Sahara was recently divorced. And maybe hungry. Joel thought he might be hungry too.

The houses across the street were built into the side of a hill, so they looked down on Joel's and Sahara's houses where the land was flat and park-like and featured many trees.

The new neighbor was short and roly-poly. He had a long and bushy white beard and mustache, long curly white hair, funny little round glasses. He was even wearing a red shirt.

Joel was so astonished to see his dream made flesh he ran the mower into a tree. The handle jammed into his stomach, making him cry out in agony.

The new neighbor waved cheerily. "Ho!" he called.

As Joel stared at what must surely be an apparition, the man seemed to dissolve and reassemble in one dimension with that same cartoon balloon issuing from his bearded mouth. "YOU'D BETTER WATCH OUT!" the pulsating words said this time.

Joel blinked and the man returned to normal dimensions. The cartoon balloon was no more. Raising a hand in another merry salute, the right jolly old elf turned and went back into his house.

Joel noticed for the first time that the shades that had been drawn since George Alencourt and his wife Jenny moved out at the beginning of the year were open now. A couple of overstuffed armchairs showed in the picture window with a small table in between. There was something on the table that Joel couldn't quite make out.

His mouth was dry, his heart ricocheting against his rib-cage. Obviously he should have worn a hat while he was out in the midday sun. Marian used to nag him to wear a hat. Sometimes he really missed her nagging.

Leaving the mower in the middle of the lawn, he returned to the house, took a beer from the refrigerator and went out to one of the Adirondack chairs on the front deck. He found himself staring fixedly at the house across the street. He thought that was a pretty dumb thing to be doing, but couldn't seem to tear his gaze away.

After a while, he saw something glinting in the middle of the picture window. Whatever had been on the table between the chairs wasn't there anymore. It was in the new neighbor's hands. Santa Claus was looking through a telescope directly at Joel!

Shocked rigid, Joel stared back, leaning forward, letting his annoyance show.

The confrontation lasted no more than ten seconds, then Santa set the telescope down and waved.

A few minutes later Joel's friend, Detective "Flat-top" Anstruther, drove into Joel's driveway. Joel gestured him onto the deck and into a companion chair. Seeing that the officer was wearing swim trunks and a T-shirt, so was obviously off-duty, Joel went to get him a beer. "I have a really weird new neighbor," he told Flat-top, pointing at the house opposite.

"Lotta weird people around," Flat-top said.

"He's a dead ringer for Santa Claus," Joel said.

Flat-top raised skeptical eyebrows.

"Short and stout, long white beard, curly white hair, little round glasses, rosy cheeks," Joel tallied.

Flat-top grinned. "Hot weather like this, everyone has rosy cheeks."

"Few minutes ago he was looking at me through a telescope," Joel told him.

The detective laughed. "Probably thinks you're weird," he said. "Let me know he starts his peepin' Tom routine on the ever-lovely Miss Sahara. Then I'll run him in."

"Something about him bothers me," Joel said. His voice sounded shaky, he realized.

"People are supposed to *like* Santa Claus," Flat-top said. He looked alertly at Joel. "How you feelin' nowadays? You gettin' over Marian leavin' you?"

"Pretty well."

"Seemed mighty depressed for a while there."

"Wouldn't you be depressed if Trish left you?"

"She'd never do that. Depends too much on the old rooty toot-toot here. Wears me out, weekends." He patted himself between the legs, looking smug.

Joel hadn't had that problem with Marian. Sex hadn't seemed to interest her.

He sighed.

Both men looked up as Sahara Brown strolled barefooted into view. She had a loose filmy wrap floating around her, supposed to be some kind of cover up for her bikini, Joel supposed. It wasn't doing a very good job. Not that he was complaining.

She sat herself down on the edge of the deck and twisted around to look at Joel and Flat-top. Almost twisted right out of her bikini top. "You notice our new neighbor yet?" Joel asked to distract himself.

She nodded.

"I was just telling Flat-top how much he looks like Santa Claus."

"You think so?"

"You kidding? He's the spitting image."

Sahara shrugged delicate shoulders, which endangered the breasts inside her bra even more. Joel forgot to breathe for a minute or two. Did he stand a chance with her? he wondered. He'd thought a couple of times since she moved in that she might be interested. He was older than her by ten years, but he still looked pretty good, he thought. A little soft around the middle maybe, but he was working on that.

"I came to ask you if that's a vegetable garden," she said, looking over at the side yard that divided her property from his.

"Used to be," Joel said. "I lost interest."

There was a time that garden had been his pride and joy. His corn alone—not to mention the carrots, the rhubarb, five kinds of lettuce, Swiss Chard, beets, green onions, potatoes, and the half barrels that were planted with every kind of herb imaginable. Marian was a gourmet cook. But that was then. This was now.

"Not much point growing a lot of veggies when you live alone," he said. "Don't plan to bother with it this year."

"We could take care of it together," Sahara suggested, looking at him over her shoulder in a way that made his stomach leap like an antelope. Okay, maybe it wasn't his stomach. "We could plant it and share the results. Or I could fix pots and pots of my great veggie soup. We could plant basil and make pesto for pasta, grow onions to caramelize—I love caramelized onions, don't you? I eat them like candy."

The pink tip of her tongue showed between her lips.

"I-I-I'll think about it," Joel managed.

Sahara shrugged again, then rose gracefully to her feet and padded away across the lawn, detouring around the garden.

Joel swallowed.

Flat-top let out a long sigh. "Joel, my man, you have it made in the shade."

"You think so?"

"Invitation written all over that little lady, you ask me. You are one lucky dawg."

"Well, I'm not accepting," Joel said. "I'm not interested in gardening."

"Out of your mind," Flat-top said.

Santa Claus developed a routine. He'd appear in his window at seven o'clock in the morning, just about the time Joel would come into the breakfast nook, his hair still curling damply from his shower. Joel would see the glint of light on the telescope lens as the old man lifted it.

Sometimes at night, Joel would wake in a sweat with that creepy feeling at the back of his neck that means someone is watching. In the dark, he'd go over to the breakfast nook window and look out. There were no streetlights in the area. But he could see light glinting on glass beyond Santa's window.

He tried making faces, sticking out his tongue like a little kid, wiggling his ears. He gave the old man the rigid digit. Nothing fazed Santa. He just held the telescope steady. Same in the evening when Joel came home from

Bartlett's Department Store.

Joel sold furniture at Bartlett's.

Joel considered putting the blinds back up at his windows. He'd taken them down after Marian left, hating the feeling they gave him of being closed in, hemmed in, suffocated. It was funny, he'd never felt claustrophobic before she left.

He thought he might just go across the street and give the old man a piece of his mind, but something held him back.

Fear.

He was *afraid* of Santa Claus, convinced he was spying on him for a reason. What reason? That was the question. Maybe the old man was a member of some kind of neighborhood morality police—got up to look like Santa for cover. Maybe he was watching to see if Joel was behaving himself, if he was doing anything with Sahara Brown. Maybe it was something else, maybe it was...

He had to laugh at himself, a big tough guy like Joel Cassidy afraid of an old geezer who looked like Santa Claus.

But there was no doubt the old fart was affecting him. The dreams kept coming. Joel began to stay awake, afraid to close his eyes. "It's probably your conscience working on you," one of the older women he worked with said when he confided in her. "Your wife left you, didn't she? You haven't had sex in how long?"

"She left Christmas Eve," Joel said, begging the question. They hadn't had sex for weeks before she left. Months maybe.

"Well there you are then," the woman said. "There's the Christmas connection. You've got the hots for this young woman and you feel guilty about it, so your mind has invented this whole Santa Claus scenario."

A guilty conscience. It sounded sort of reasonable. He certainly had one of those. Though he hadn't *done* anything with Sahara even if he had thought about it. Until

Marian left him, he'd respected his wedding vows. He supposed he was just naturally the faithful kind. Fat lot of good it had done him.

It would be a pretty far-out coincidence, he thought, trying to make a joke out of the situation—a sex-kitten like Sahara Brown moving into the neighborhood and getting interested in Joel Cassidy just when some crazy Santa Claus clone started spying on him awake and asleep.

"He's a birder," Detective Flat-top Anstruther said next time he came by to visit Joel. "Told me there's some kind of yellow-shafted flicker doesn't usually appear in these parts. Showed up in that big fir tree behind your garage. Old guy wants to complete his life list before he croaks. Birders get fanatical like that. Hell, I've seen birders down by the creek with their "bins" as they call 'em, at four o'clock in the mornin'."

A life list, Joel thought. Yeah. He'd seen the old guy writing stuff down while he sat in his chair in the window.

A *birder*. Joel felt relieved. He'd been in danger of becoming unhinged, he thought.

"What you need, my boy," Flat-top said, "is a good lay. Want my advice, forget about Santa, give Miss Sahara a break. No doubt about it, she thinks you are hot!"

The more he thought about it, the more Joel liked the sound of that. The next time he saw Sahara outside her house—she was extracting the evening newspaper from her box—he ambled over and remarked on the continued warm weather.

"If we're going to work on that veggie garden, we're going to have to do it soon," Sahara said. "Doesn't look like there's any danger of frost. What do you say I come over and we start turning the soil over tomorrow? It's Saturday. You're off on Saturdays, aren't you? So am I. In the evening, we can get out the catalogs and go over them."

An image of Sahara sitting close to him on the living room sofa, her wildly curling hair shining in the lamplight, made Joel's throat get tight.

"We can do it together," she said, looking up at him through her eyelashes.

The way she said "do it" left no room for doubt in his mind. She was hot for him, just like Flat-top had said.

But what if Santa saw them together?

Why should he care? Santa was a birder. It was his own guilty conscience that had made him imagine Santa Claus was spying on him.

But what if Santa Claus saw him doing what he would have to do tonight, before Sahara came over tomorrow?

There was a little black moon on the calendar for tonight, he remembered abruptly. There would be no light. And there were several trees between the garden and the part of the property that faced Santa Claus's house.

Sahara was waiting for an answer.

"Okay," Joel said through a catch in his throat. "Tomorrow it is."

Just to be on the safe side, he waited until he was sure Santa Claus and Sahara had gone to bed. When not a glimmer of light showed in the windows across the street or in the house next door, he crept into the side yard carrying a spade. All he had to do was check to see how far he had dug down last time. He had been in such a hurry, he couldn't remember. If he had dug down far enough, he might not have to do anything at all.

Sticking the spade gingerly in the middle of the garden, he pushed down with one foot. And struck something. Carefully he scraped away soil until he could reach down and touch the obstruction, make sure it was what he thought it was.

Damn. That's what he'd been afraid of. He hadn't gone down far enough. Now he'd have to make other arrangements. Leaning on the spade, he began to conceive a plan. First he would dig a hole in the back yard, then come back here and...

The flashlight shining in his face took him completely by surprise. "The old man said you'd crack," Flat-top Anstruther said.

"He sure did," Sahara added. "The old man's terrific on psychology."

While Joel stood there frozen like a bug pinned to a board, Flat-top shone his flashlight on the ground. Marian's left hand and arm had decomposed quite a bit.

"Looks like Marian's ring," Flat-top said.

Joel nodded.

"I didn't want to believe you'd killed her," Flat-top said. "You had that letter from her saying she was leavin' you. She'd written thank you notes to Trish, times we had you two over to dinner, so I knew it was her handwritin'."

He paused. "Several people saw Marian goin' off in a taxi. The ticket seller at the train station remembered her buyin' a ticket. How'd you do it?"

"You've no cause to think I did it," Joel said. He thought rapidly. "Someone telephoned me. Some anonymous person. He called a little while ago and said he'd killed her and buried her here. I was just checking when..."

"Lame, Joel, very lame." Flat-top laughed. "The old guy lives across the street saw you bury her Christmas Eve, see. He was in the area, visitin' some people, just happened to see you as he went by."

"He really is Santa Claus," Joel said dully.

"Nah!" Flat-top said. "His name's something real simple. Nick Smith, Nick Jones, something like that."

"Nicholas," Joel said. "*Saint* Nicholas."

The detective's voice toughened up. "Okay, Joel, how about getting it off your chest? You'll feel better. This is your old friend Flat-top. You can tell *me*. How'd you do it?"

There didn't seem much point to holding out any longer.

"I came home early that night," Joel said. "It was a

slow day at the store. I found the letter minutes after Marian left. She'd made it easy, said what train she was catching. She was standing in front of those big rhododendron bushes side of the platform. Nobody saw me. I pulled her back into the woods and strangled her. Went back for her suitcase. She had no *right* to leave me. I was her *husband*. She had no *right*. Anybody left, it should have been *me*. Made me real mad, her leaving me."

"So then you brought her back here and buried her in your vegetable garden."

Joel realized Sahara was no longer among those present. He reckoned he wasn't going to get to sit with her in the lamplight after all.

He sighed. "Like I said, I was spitting mad. Didn't really think it all out. But it worked pretty good, I guess. Until now."

"That old guy across the street called me a couple weeks ago to say he'd seen you bury her," Flat-top explained. "Said he'd have called sooner but he'd worked overtime all durin' the holidays and got worn out. He just got rested up. Said he'd figured out how to get you to trap yourself. So there'd be no doubt it was you did it. Asked me to co-operate. Guess he must have brought Sahara into it too."

"He's Santa Claus," Joel said. "Maybe she's Mrs. Claus."

Flat-top laughed. "She don't look like no Mrs. Claus I ever saw, but if that's the way you want to believe it, you go right ahead."

He stopped laughing abruptly. "You have the right to remain silent and to refuse to answer questions," he intoned in an official sounding voice.

Joel had stopped listening. There was a new sound in the air. A whooshing sound that he remembered hearing the night he buried Marian. A sound like the beating wings of a flock of geese heading north for the summer, a sound like the wind.

He looked up. Directly above his head a dark shadow

was passing over—a dark shadow that was shaped remarkably like a sleigh.

"...anything you say can and will be used against you," Flat-top was saying now, apparently unaware of the sleigh above their heads.

In the front seat next to Santa sat Sahara, her wonderful hair blowing in the wind. They both waved cheerily. As they did so, they seemed to turn and dissolve and become one-dimensional like cardboard cutouts, their right arms held stiffly aloft. There was a cartoon balloon coming out of Santa Claus's mouth, a single word in it pulsating with light.

"HO!" it said.

MADRAS

Craig Lesley

*During the Cold War, I volunteered for the Civil Air Patrol in
Madras, Oregon, and I always wanted to write about that wacky
experience. Our duty was to make certain that no Russian planes
attacked Madras or the tiny communities around it. Metolius had
about two hundred people and two big tin-roofed potato storage sheds
we believed the Russians wanted to bomb as part of a plan to
"starve" Oregon. Of course, this was all hysteria, but some paranoids
were going through 33-rpm records tossing out any with references to
"red" including "Red Sails in the Sunset".*

I SPENT TWO YEARS in the late 1950s making America
safe for democracy by keeping a vigilant eye out for enemy
planes—North Korean and Russian piloted Migs that
might be threatening Oregon's interior near Madras.
Tuesdays and Thursdays after school, my friend Tub Hobson
and I stood on the flat roof of the Madras Fire Department
scanning the horizon for hostiles.

With the naked eye, and a single pair of cloudy
binoculars traded back and forth, we repeatedly swept all
four quadrants, taking no chances enemy planes would

sneak by us to attack Culver, Gateway, or God help us, open fire on Madras itself. Our Boy Scout leader had warned that even seemingly harmless places like Metolius were prime targets, given the fact that they grew and stored potatoes there. He told of starvation during the Irish potato famines and how Stalin starved the Ukrainians by taking away their potatoes. Now our enemies threatened Central Oregon's spuds. I was convinced by the leader's speech but Hobson was more skeptical.

"Hairballs," he whispered.

In spite of our best intentions, strict discipline faltered in about an hour. By that time my eyes stung from staring over Mt. Jefferson, Mt. Bachelor, Three-Fingered Jack, and the Three Sisters, roughly the directions of North Korea and Russia, if you drew a line toward infinity.

Hob slugged me hard in the shoulder. "Don't rub it," he challenged.

His fists were bigger than mine and he already had grown the beginnings of a moustache.

"I think I felt a mosquito," I said but didn't rub it, even though my shoulder hurt like hell.

"I can throw farther than you can," Tub said.

"Not unless the bears come out of the woods."

"Betcha I can."

Dozens of rocks, some large as apples, mysteriously appeared on the flat composition roof before we manned each shift. We figured other high-schoolers, probably the "hoods," threw them up in a night ritual. Our task was to throw them off aiming for the city fire department's pumper truck parked in a gravel back lot half a block away.

My shoulder remained sore after Tub's slug, but I limbered up and selected a baseball-sized rock. To gain momentum, I ran toward the roof's edge, then flung the rock hard and high. It clanged off the truck's water tank.

Imitating the voice of a baseball announcer, I spoke: "Tub Hobson rounds third and Lesley makes the throw from deep center field. It's going to be awfully close, folks, but he's called out at the plate. What a major-league throw!"

"Pure blind luck, you throwing that far." Tub spit on his right palm, wound up, and threw with a mighty oomph.

The rock fell short.

Cupping my hand behind my ear, I asked, "Did you hear a clunk, Tub? Maybe I'm getting deaf."

Disgusted, he thrust his hands in his pockets and shrugged. "Hey, no kidding. How come you always out throw me, Lesley? You got smaller arms and skinnier shoulders." He seemed genuinely puzzled.

"Physics," I said.

"Physics?"

"Remember, you got a C in Mr. Johnson's physics class and I got an A. Momentum and thrust, Tub. Angle of trajectory. Keep that in mind."

"Weenie Arm!"

In that five minutes or so while we goofed off, I suppose a plane or two could have snuck by unnoticed, but fortunately, they didn't.

What did fly across the Madras skies during our watch? A yellow biplane crop-duster, numerous magpies, a confused pheasant that wandered into town and dodged sparse traffic. Closer to the earth, we also spotted a few wobbly drunks escorted by the police from the Shangri-La Bar to the city lockup, where they idled until their red-faced wives reclaimed them.

Thank heavens no enemy planes threatened Madras on our watch. In those days, the city police car had no radio (tight budget), so if an emergency occurred, Madge Frudgett, the dispatcher, lit a red beacon on top of the firehouse. The light was visible from anywhere in Madras—except the dark, smoky bars. When he saw the light, Herb Vibbert, the officer on duty, would stop at a house, ask to borrow their phone, and call in to see what was happening. All of this took time.

While Tub and I were freezing in the winter, baking in the summer, the light flashed only a few emergencies, but most were routine: stolen bicycles, cows breaking through fences, pregnant women going into early labor. Whoever spotted the flashing light first got to punch the other volunteer squarely in the shoulder and say, "Don't rub it." Then add, "Do you see any enemy planes, Horse Face?"

Most shifts were uneventful outside of the throwing and punching. For the last hour of the shift, I gazed toward the snow-capped beauty of the Cascades—the jagged crest of Three-Fingered Jack, the rugged beauty of Broken Top —and hiking alpine meadows filled with wildflowers.

Shifting my eyes, I'd watch the sunlight glinting off the tin potato shed roofs at Metolius and realize they did make ideal targets. Strengthened by my resolve to complete my duty, I'd stare hard at the sky another twenty minutes until black dots danced before my eyes. But even so, my mind wandered to my Uncle Oscar's sporting goods store and all the equipment I planned to buy with summer earnings.

Finally, Madge would crunch out onto the gravel parking lot to announce that our shift was over and invite us for cookies and Kool-Aid in the dispatch room. We descended the shaky ladder while two more eager Civil Air Patrol volunteers headed for the roof.

After scarfing the drinks and sticking extra Snicker-doodles into our pockets, Tub and I made our way toward separate homes, confident we had kept Madras safe for another three hours. We parted at the county jail where sad-eyed men gestured out the bars, begging smokes.

"See you tomorrow, Bacteria-Breath," Tub said.

"Same to you but more of it," I answered. I sauntered home, secretly pleased with his friendship and confident that any major league scouts visiting Madras would covet my throwing arm. Once again, Tub and I had guaranteed that Central Oregon was safe from invaders.

Many years later, when the Metolius potato sheds finally did collapse, no one could discern a reason. Old age, gravity, saboteurs. No potatoes had inhabited the sheds for years, but a few transients had been reported taking up residency.

Earl Cordes, Jefferson County Fire Chief, drove out the five miles in response to a call from the sheriff's office. According to the story featured in the Madras *Pioneer*, Cordes yelled into the collapsed building (a dangerous mess), but got no response. "So far I've received no reply," he told the paper. "So they're either unconscious, dead, or not there."

I wonder what became of the so-called transients. Perhaps they were saboteurs, following sinister orders from a foreign power. Were they agents from Cuba, North Korea, the former USSR?

Maybe Cordes is right. "Unconscious," "dead," or "not there" implies no one is threatening Central Oregon, but I'm not so easily convinced. Growing up with full knowledge of the Red menace, I know how sneaky those Commies can be. Even now, they could be hiding in seed carrots, the bluegrass fields, or lurking in the mint just waiting for us to lower our guard.

CITIES OF GOLD

Kathleen Alcalá

Serena Diamond is the young adult child of immigrants who grows up near Los Angeles. The title refers to the idealized places each of us keeps in her heart, whether living in Seattle, Los Angeles, New Mexico, or Tuva.

"WHAT DO YOU THINK you want?" asked Devi.

"A house by the beach. Maybe kids. I don't know."

"Do you want a husband to go with the kids?"

"Oh, I suppose so. Do I have to live with him?"

Devi threw a gum wrapper at her. "That's the general idea. Two kids, a house, a dog. The dad lives with you. You are married and have dinner at your parents house once a week and the guys watch football."

Serena tried to imagine this. "Oh, please. What about you? Your family lives all over the world."

"When the time comes, I will consult an astrologer," Devi intoned, dramatically raising her hands. Her voice dropped to assume a deep, mysterious tone, "who will find me my prince, the one with whose destiny mine is entwined." She clasped her hands together over her heart.

"You're kidding, right?" Serena was never quite sure with Devi, since her family was from India.

"Who knows? It might be as good a way as any to get married. It worked for my parents."

"Yeah, but—that was different. That was in another country and everything."

"How did your parents get together?" asked Devi in a normal voice.

Serena shrugged. "I don't know. I think my dad went to work for my mom's father. And her dad thought he was okay for her. . ."

Devi pointed at her. "See...!"

"But that was different too!" interrupted Serena. "That was a long time ago. Things are different now."

"Yeah," said Devi. She didn't sound happy or sad. "Let's go get some lunch. I'm starving."

"Let's pick up some Cokes and go to my grandma's. I haven't seen her recently. She'll feed us."

"Yeah, but I can't eat anything she fixes," said Devi.

Devi was sporadically vegetarian. Serena had seen her eat lobster before, even though Serena herself thought it tasted gross.

"Okay, let's pick up drinks and a salad for you and go see my grandma."

Abuela was in her tiny back yard when they pulled up, smoking, and throwing scraps of lettuce to her pet duck. In spite of everything people said to her, Abuela would not give up smoking. She was about a million years old. The cement bench on which she sat was surrounded by a riot of herbs and flowers.

Patito squawked loudly upon seeing Serena and waddled over to her. The pet duck loved Serena. "This duck is getting big," she cooed to it as the duck nibbled at her hair. "*Qué gordito.*"

"I swear, Serena," said Devi. "I have never seen anything

like this duck. It acts like a dog or something with you."

Serena exchanged *abrazos* with her grandmother, and Devi did as well. Then Abuela seated herself carefully on her bench and began to speak in formal cadences to Serena. Serena nodded and smiled, sometimes answering "*Sí,*" or shrugging and saying "*No sé,*" as her grandmother spoke. Serena barely understood any Spanish, and her grandmother spoke no English, but Serena loved to hear her talk.

Serena was sure that her grandmother was imparting all of her love and the wisdom of the ages, and if she could only understand her, life would be easier. Serena knew that her grandmother had lived a hard life, giving birth to children who did not live, that Uncle Mike had died in Korea. Somehow, Serena felt that her grandmother's values were less prosaic, that she understood Serena's own longings and desperations, her passion, in a way that her parents refused to acknowledge. If they had ever felt passion, for each other or for anything else, Serena thought, it had long been damped down by the expectations of a middle class life. 'What will the neighbors think?' had long superseded 'What do I need to feel alive?'

Devi sat on the grass and fed bits of her salad to the duck. It made wonderful contented noises, and Devi giggled and tried to pet it.

Finally, Abuela jumped up and offered them some food. "*Es hora de comer!*" she said.

Abuela always had some cooked beans in a pot on her ancient, dinky stove. She heated oil in a skillet and dipped beans out of the pot, smashing them onto the hot skillet to make refritos. Serena's stomach grumbled as she walked around the tiny living room, examining the old photos and doilies and miniature paintings from places she would never visit. Her grandmother kept the drapes closed, so that it was cool and dark.

She paused at a photo of her grandparents. She had heard all her life that her grandfather had been either a horrible drunk or a wonderful man. Maybe he had been a wonderful man when he wasn't drunk. They both looked serious in the photo, the man holding his hat, the woman with her carefully marcelled hair. The hairdo was held in place with a diamond clip, and Serena wondered if her grandmother still had it. She was sure it wasn't made of real diamonds, but she wanted to own it someday.

Six months earlier, she had had a small diamond tattooed on her ankle. Devi had gone with her. It was very tasteful, she thought, a dot design that resembled henna, with lines that radiated from the longer points of the diamonds. The tattoo artist in Venice Beach, Veronikka, designed it especially for her.

When Julio saw it, his lip curled up in that way he had. "It looks…"

"Tacky?" said Serena at the same time that he said "Cheap."

She knew that he wouldn't like it. That's why she didn't tell him she was going to do it. Still, she didn't expect him to act that bad. Serena had gotten up and left.

Julio was going to end up just like those other guys from school, marrying the blonde trophy wife who would look good at company receptions. Now he acted like he was better than she was, just because he had gone to law school. She remembered when he couldn't tell which end of a tie was supposed to be on top.

Serena's grandmother called her to sit at the card table that served as her dining room, placed so that it extended from the kitchen into the living room. Abuela herself refused to sit down, preferring to hover by the stove where she turned tortillas and brought them hot and steaming to Serena. Abuela ate holding a plate in one hand, in bits and pieces, like the duck.

Devi came in from the yard, her face flushed. "It's getting hot out there," she said. "Maybe we should go to the beach."

"That sounds nice," said Serena. "Sit down and eat something. You'll offend grandma if you don't."

Devi sat down and accepted a plain corn tortilla. She sucked at the straw in her drink until she made noises at the bottom. Abuela took her glass of ice and refilled it from the tap.

"Thanks!" said Devi.

"De nada."

"De nada," Devi repeated, then looked uncertainly at Serena.

"That means, you're welcome," said Serena. "Well, really it means, it's nothing, but it means the same thing."

Serena's grandmother had liked the tattoo right away. "Ah, *un diamante!*' she said. Serena's father had changed his name when he went in the Army during World War II.

"Otherwise, they would have thought I was Italian," he had said. "This way, everyone can say it and spell it."

But Abuela's name was still Diamante—Anita Diamante, *"como la joya,"* she would add, like the gem.

Suddenly there was a commotion outside—brakes squealing and a dog barking.

"Patito!" said Abuela. *"Qué paso con* Patito?"

They all ran outside. Sure enough, the duck had gotten out of the yard. It had attracted the attention of one of the many loose mutts in the neighborhood and been chased into the street. Now the duck quacked plaintively, running in frantic circles with traffic stopped in both directions.

Serena tried to shoo the dog off from where it stood barking and whining, leery of the cars, but attracted by its prey.

Abuela took her apron off over her head and holding it out in her hands, began to approach Patito, making soothing, clucking noises, oblivious to the cars and their impatient drivers. Just as she was closing in on the duck, a black car came gunning down the curb lane, trying to get around the stalled traffic. The duck noisily became airborne.

"Grandma, no!" screamed Serena, running back across the street, heedless of her own safety. She saw her grandmother fall. The noisy black car, windows tinted dark, bass notes thumping, ripped by, barely missing Serena's car parked at the curb as it swerved back into a through lane.

"Grandma!" yelled Serena. By now, the car nearest to her grandmother had stopped, people were leaning out of their cars to see what was going on, and neighbors watering their lawns were putting down their hoses and coming over. A pack of children materialized out of nowhere.

Devi knelt by Serena's grandmother.

"Are you okay?" she asked softly.

The old woman looked dazed, but sat up. Dried grass clung to her hair and the side of her face.

"Sí, estoy bien," she said.

"Are you hurt?" asked Serena. "Are you okay? Did the car hit her?" she said to Devi.

"She jumped out of the way." Devi looked as shook up as Abuela.

Serena and Devi helped Abuela to her feet. Satisfied that there were no permanent casualties, the drivers got back in their cars and kept driving.

"Can you look for my Grandma's duck?" Serena asked the children, as much to get rid of them as find the duck. "If you find it, just tell me where it is. Don't try to catch it, or it will get too scared." A neighbor handed Devi the balled-up apron, grimy with road grit from the street.

The children took off chattering. Serena figured they would scare it to death anyway, even if it wasn't already flattened. But she wanted to get her grandmother in the house and make sure she was okay.

They took Abuela into her bedroom and made her lie down. Serena spread one of the crocheted afghans over her legs, and brought her a glass of water. Soon she was asleep.

Devi had hardly said a word this whole time. She walked into the living room and sat wide-eyed on the green couch with lace doilies on each arm.

"It's my fault," she said.

"What is?" asked Serena.

"I think I left the gate open when we first came in."

"Don't be silly," said Serena. "That duck's always getting out. We all forgot about it. She usually puts it in a cage by the side of the house when she's not outside with it."

A little later, there was a shy knock on the front door. Only strangers came to the front door, while everyone else came around through the back garden.

Serena tried to open the door, which stuck. She tugged harder, and the dim little room was flooded with bright light as the door popped open.

A shy girl in a red ruffled top and pants stood there chewing on the tip of her ponytail. She was about seven. When she saw Serena, she turned and looked up to the young man behind her. He looked like he was about twenty. A small boy clung to his pant leg.

"Go ahead, *mija*, tell her," he said. "About the duck." Serena realized he was the father of the children, and had to be a little older.

The girl turned her big eyes back to Serena and said, in a husky voice, "We found the duck."

Serena knelt down on the porch. The girl had tiny gold hoops in her ears. "You did?" She glanced up to the father, who nodded encouragingly. "Is it okay?"

"Yeah," said the girl, "It's in a bathtub."

"Just a second," said Serena. "I'll be right there." She closed the door without latching it.

"Will you stay with my grandma while I get the duck?" she asked Devi.

"Of course," she said. "Where is it?"

"I don't know," said Serena. "Close, I hope."

Serena grabbed a handful of candy from the bowl on

the kitchen counter before following the little girl and her father outside. More children waited on the sidewalk. They walked down to the end of the block to cross the busy street. Even at the light, the cars were reluctant to stop for them. She took the little girl's hand, and the man picked up his little boy. Only Serena and the girl's family crossed.

On the other side, they entered a neighborhood that was a little quieter, with big shade trees. The houses were old, but fixed up. "I can't believe Patito came this far," said Serena.

"Birds can be pretty smart," said the dad. He seemed as shy as his daughter. Serena liked that.

They walked almost another block before turning up a driveway. There was a camper truck parked outside the garage.

"I take care of this house when the people are away," explained the father. "They're in Tucson right now."

He unlatched the gate in a chain link fence and they entered the backyard. It was an oasis of green. Serena heard a grating noise.

"Is that a frog?" she asked.

"Yup, a big one."

They followed cement stepping stones through big clumps of pampas grass and birds of paradise. Serena stopped to look at the lettering on one of them. "Freddie Junior," she read out loud. "September 12, 1989."

"Those are their grandkids. There's a step for each one, with their birthdays."

There were a lot of them. The stepping stones led to a small, perfectly oval pond. When Serena saw the spigot and handles at one end, she realized that it was a bathtub set into the ground. It was surrounded by ferns and flowering plants. "It *is* a bathtub," she said. The little girl giggled.

Patito was fast asleep on the other side, his head tucked under a wing. He looked like an extra in a movie. One about rajas and sheiks and lonely princesses and lost cities of gold.

"I hate to wake him," said Serena. "He's had a big day."

"How are you planning to get him back?"

"I don't know," she said. "Maybe if we had a box."

"I can get you one," said the man, and left with his little boy, who had not said a word the whole time Serena had been with them. The little girl stayed behind with Serena, still clinging to her hand.

"What's your name?" asked Serena softly. She did not want the duck to wake up and get excited.

"Jasmin," said the girl.

"Jasmin? Like in Aladdin?"

The girl nodded. She was staring up at Serena. "You're pretty," she said.

Serena smiled. She reached into her pocket and held out a candy on her palm as though offering it to a small animal. The girl hesitated, then took it slowly, letting go of Serena's hand to unwrap it and pop it into her mouth.

The dad and his little boy returned with a big cardboard box. This time the duck woke up and began pacing uneasily, talking to itself in low quacks.

"Patito…" said Serena soothingly, hoping that her voice would lure the duck. Patito twitched his tail, but did not cross the pond to where she stood. The duck eyed the others nervously.

Finally, the father stepped across the pond to where the duck stood between the water and the back fence, grabbing it around the middle before it could react. It quacked and struggled madly, but despite almost losing his balance and dipping his foot into the tub, the man didn't let go.

Serena held the box open while he put Patito inside. As soon as the top was folded shut, the duck quieted.

"That should do it," the man said. "I can carry it back for you."

151

"Oh no, thanks," said Serena "You've done enough already. And now you're soaked."

The man looked at his squishy tennis shoe and smiled ruefully. Serena felt a slight surge inside. What would it be like to be married to a man like this, to have a little boy and a daughter named Jasmin?

"My grandma will be really happy to get her duck back. Thanks," she said, "and thank you, Jasmin, for helping."

Serena carried the cardboard box carefully in front of her. Across the busy street, the jumping children greeted her with shrieks and howls, causing the duck to shift uneasily in the dark confines of the box. Serena handed out the rest of the candy, but refused to open the box and show them the duck.

"It's tired," she said. "It's taking a little nap." She was afraid it would get loose again.

"It's dead, isn't it?" said a little boy.

"No," said Serena, "listen." She set the box on the hot sidewalk. The children quieted enough to hear the duck shuffling and making small noises in the box.

"It's alive!" they whispered gleefully to each other. "It's alive!"

Serena carried the box the rest of the way to her grandmother's. At the gate, the children waved goodbye and Serena carried the box around the side of the house to where her grandmother kept a small mesh-wire pen. It was as much to protect the duck from dogs as to keep it from escaping. She opened the door to the cage and tipped the box on its side.

Patito quacked loudly, ruffling his feathers, but seemed relieved to be in familiar surroundings. Serena was careful to fasten the wire that held the door shut. "There you go, Patito." She turned on the hose and sprayed some water on the duck, making sure to fill its bowl.

Letting herself in the back door, Serena felt hot and itchy. "Devi?" she called.

"Here," she answered. Devi was in the kitchen with Serena's grandmother, drying dishes. Her grandmother had changed into a fresh housedress.

"*Mira.*" said the old woman, lifting her hem like a mischievous schoolgirl to show a long, dark bruise on her leg.

"*Ay,* Abuela," said Serena. "*¿Quieres ir al doctor?*"

"No," her grandmother said gesturing emphatically with her hands. "*Estoy bien. No mas tengo magulladura.*"

"There's a scrape on her arm," said Devi. "But she let me wash it off. I think she's okay." Devi looked better now, relieved.

Serena looked at the frail skin on her grandmother's arm. This could have been really bad, she thought. "I'm just going to call my dad, okay?" Serena dialed her parents number. It was late afternoon by now, and no one answered. She hung up. "They're probably at Costco."

"*Mira,*" said Serena, imitating her grandmother. She took Abuela's good arm and led her outside. The old woman limped a little. Serena showed her the duck, quacking to itself in the little pen.

Her grandmother clapped her hands in delight. "*¡Ay, qué bueno!*" she said. "*Se volvio mi* Patito, *gracias a Dios!*"

She said some more things that Serena didn't understand.

"We've got to go now," said Serena. She got her purse and keys from inside the house, "Come on, Devi," she said.

"Is your grandmother going to be alright?" asked Devi.

"I think so. She's tough," said Serena. "I'll have my dad check on her later. He'll want to."

In Serena's car, Devi fiddled with the CD player. "Well, it's too late to go to the beach," she said. "What do you want to do?"

"Don't you have a date later?" asked Serena. "You always have a date."

"I'm mad at Kevin," she said. "He's two-timing me."

"Like you don't two-time him?" said Serena, laughing.

"That's different," said Devi. "That's just for fun. This girl really wants him. A friend told me."

"Some friend."

"Let's see a movie," said Devi. "A kung-fu gut buster."

"You like those, don't you?"

"Yeah, I need something loud to get over the excitement at your grandmother's."

Serena glanced over at Devi. "Look, it's not your fault, okay? She's just fine. Even the duck is fine, although Patito will definitely end up paté someday."

Devi cranked up the CD player, and they joined a long line of cars snaking its way over the Hollywood Hills.

"Let's get one of those magazines," said Serena, "and look up our horoscopes."

"Forget it," said Devi. "I saw the way you looked at that guy, the one with the little girl. He's taken."

"I know," said Serena wistfully. She downshifted as traffic slowed, squinting at the road ahead, as though trying to see into the future. "I know."

DINNER WITH VLAD

Robert Ferrigno

Arturo, against his wife's wishes, brings Vlad home for dinner. While the wife is creeped out by Vlad, the children relate to him, recognizing him as a damaged child who never had a chance.

VLAD KEPT his arms in his lap as Fortuna, Arturo's wife, served him a slice of hot apple pie, à la mode. He was embarrassed at the cysts that had erupted on his forearms in the last few weeks, like marbles half-buried in his flesh. He should have worn a long-sleeved shirt, he thought, watching the ice cream slide off the pie crust. He caught Fortuna staring at his arms. "It's not catching," he said. "I promise."

Fortuna ignored him, served her four children pie, then excused herself.

"What's your hurry?" demanded Arturo.

"I have to plan the sixth grade awards banquet," said Fortuna, a short, stout woman with gray hair cut short and a gold Rolex that Armando had taken off a cocaine dealer last year. The watch looked very good on her thick wrist.

"Should I let Preston graduate in silence?"

Arturo waved her away.

"The pie is really good," Vlad called to Fortuna.

Arturo checked the security monitors. It was a reflex by now. He had a bank of six monitors in every room of the house, and on the balconies too. Six views of the surrounding area, the routes anyone wishing to harm him, or his family would have to take. They lived in a private, gated community in south county. The name on the deed and all utilities was an offshore holding company Arturo had set up. The four children went to a private school, using his wife's maiden name. He changed cars at least twice before he came home at night. There had never been any sign, not the slightest indication that any of their enemies knew where he lived, but Arturo checked his monitors about as often as he blinked.

Vlad licked ice cream off the side of his mouth, his napkin untouched.

"Your arm bumps are really cool, Vlad," said Preston, a slender, neatly-dressed boy with thick glasses and skin the color of a Hershey's chocolate bar.

Vlad blushed.

"Don't say *cool*. It's low class." Arturo wore a suit and tie, gold cufflinks in the shape of an American flag, his hair pomaded and stiff.

"Cool," Hillary said softly. She was eight, short and stocky as her parents, her hair in a long, shiny braid. She wore a ruffled, yellow frock from the store at Fashion Island that specialized in Victorian era clothes. Good girl clothes, Vlad had thought when Arturo took him there. She touched Vlad's bumps. "You look like the Bionic Man."

"I like that show," said Vlad.

"Me too," said Hillary.

"They don't even make that *stupid* show anymore," said Jacqueline, Hillary's twin, wearing the identical yellow frock. She was a good Catholic, and the only one of the

156

children who shared her mother's distaste for Vlad. "It got canceled."

Vlad went to eat another bite of pie, but his fork stopped halfway to his mouth. He struggled to move his hand, ice cream dripping onto the table cloth, finally drew the fork smoothly into his mouth. "Delicious," he said, hoping no one had noticed.

"I'm doing a report on Romania," said Sean, Arturo's oldest son, a strapping boy of fifteen, taller than his father, handsome, with quiet eyes, his black hair cut short. A chess player, and starter on the lacrosse team, president of the honor society.

Vlad nodded, pleased.

"Don't be bothering Vlad about that," said Arturo.

"I don't mind," said Vlad.

"Amnesty International says that the old dictator— the one who got killed..."

"Ceaucesque," said Vlad.

"That's a *stupid* name," said Jacqueline.

"Ceaucesque had his best scientists working to create supermen or supersoldiers," said Sean, ignoring his sister, excited now, eyes bright. "They did some of the first recombinant DNA research, and selective breeding experiments. All kinds of drugs were given to the children, and they performed all kinds of illegal operations on them."

Vlad carefully set down his fork. He could not feel the tips of his fingers. It was as if they had been amputated. He felt the tingling in his hands more and more often lately.

"The articles I read said that even though the people of Romania were poor and starving, no expense was spared on these—special kids or whatever they were called," said Sean.

"They were called the New Ones," Vlad said quietly.

"Time for homework," said Arturo.

Vlad leaned towards Sean. "The scientists were very diligent, very motivated, and they had the best equipment in the world, but, they were *experimenting*. You know what that means, yes?"

"It means that the scientists didn't know what was going to happen," said Hillary, seated beside him, listening to every word that was said.

"That's right," said Vlad. "The scientists had high hopes, and were very successful, all things considered, but it would have taken *decades*, not years, to achieve their goal, generations and generations of research. They didn't have enough time. When the regime was overthrown, the scientists had really only taken the first few steps into creating the New Ones. First steps are always—wobbly. That's the right word, I think." Arturo's children nodded, even Jacqueline. "Those New Ones who reached adulthood—they were wobbly."

Hillary patted his hand. "You don't seem wobbly to me."

Vlad could feel his fingertips again, but he didn't respond, waited until she took her hand away. "The scientists didn't really think we needed all the—things that clutter up the rest of you. Certain feelings—certain emotions were deemed expendable. Counter-productive, even."

Sean stared down at the remnants of his dessert. Preston folded his hands in his lap. Jacqueline played with her braid, oblivious.

"It's okay." Vlad could see tears in Hillary's eyes. "I don't mind."

Arturo looked away from the monitors, noticed the silence in the dining room. "Children. *Homework.*"

VLAD AND ARTURO
UNDER THE STARS

Robert Ferrigno

*Vlad and Arturo that same evening, lying in Arturo's yard
and looking up at the stars.*

"THAT THING THAT HAPPENED to you at dinner...." Arturo watched Vlad lying on the grass, looking up at the stars. "You not being able to move your hand—has that happened before?"

Vlad didn't answer, his fingers stroking the long Bermuda as though it were the pelt of a wild animal. The grass was lush and green and freshly mowed, rolled every year and not a weed in it. Arturo had a Japanese man come in every week to trim the grass, clip the hedges, feed the plants, spray for insects. Arturo refused to let his children see other Hispanics doing landscaping. His own father had worked for a lawn service, worked twelve hours a day; Arturo's father had cracked nails, and a stooped back, his brown face creased like an old baseball mitt.

"Has this thing with your hand happened before?"

repeated Arturo.

"I love your grass, Arturo. I never felt such soft grass."

"You should go to a doctor. Get checked out."

"I have seen enough doctors." Vlad raised himself up on one elbow. "Don't worry. I won't let you down."

"I'm not worried about myself. I'm worried about *you*."

Vlad lay back. His smile was silver in the moonlight.

Arturo looked out over the valley. He had the biggest lot in the gated community, a double lot, a full-acre high on the hilltop overlooking the lowlands. He came out here every night after dinner while his wife put the younger children to bed, just sat out here and listened to the crickets and the owls and the coyotes, all the animals of his youth, listening to them again, and it was all different now. Hillary started playing piano from the front room, a piece by Bach, if he remembered correctly. Arturo had no ear for music himself, not this European symphonic music at any rate, but he liked hearing Hillary play, liked watching her sit at the keyboard, posture perfect, eyes closed as her fingers flew. All his children took music lessons, math lessons, computer lessons, etiquette lessons. They had athletic training too, but not baseball or basketball. Austin and Sean played lacrosse and squash and tennis, while Hillary and Jacqueline swam and took horseback riding, dressage, of course, activities which would prepare them for the world he envisioned them dominating. Private schools, and later, private universities, where their lessons would be put to good use. No one would ever mistake them for hired help.

"How are your stocks?" said Vlad.

"Don't talk to me about the market."

"They say on TV that things will come back."

"They say a lot of bullshit on TV. I'd have been better off watching cartoons with you than the business channel."

Vlad pressed himself into the earth, wanting to sink

down, down, down to the very center, the molten core where dragons were birthed. "Dinner was very good tonight. I liked the chicken with the cheese."

"That's chicken cordon bleu."

"Chicken cording...?"

"It's French for chicken with cheese. My kids have never had a burrito in their life."

"I like burritos."

"I like burritos too, but I don't want my kids eating that kind of food." Arturo fingered the knot in his necktie. "You should find a nice girl to cook for you...."

"A nice girl wouldn't have anything to do with me."

Arturo didn't want to argue. They listened to the crickets, drifting on the raucous love song. If Arturo hadn't quit smoking, it would have been a perfect time to light up a Cuban, bask in the redolent smoke, but he *had* quit tobacco, along with fried foods, and sweets. Sometimes he thought there was too high a price for wanting to live forever.

"I think your wife is getting used to me," Vlad said.

"There's nothing to get used to. You're my friend."

"At the beginning...one time after dinner, I saw her throw away the silverware I had used. The plate and the silverware, right into the trash."

"You should have told me." Arturo glanced toward the house. Fortuna would have gone to bed, but he was going to wake her when Vlad went home. "You feeling okay?"

Vlad lay motionless on the grass.

"No more nosebleeds?"

"Nosebleeds aren't so bad." Vlad looked up at Arturo. "I have had nosebleeds since I was a child. We all did." He plucked a single blade of grass, stroked his cheek with it. "The doctors said it was to be expected."

Arturo shook his head. "I never even saw a doctor until I was thirteen...fourteen, something like that, and then all he did was look down my throat and give me a shot."

"Just one shot?"

"Hurt like crazy. I wanted to tear his eyes out."

Vlad laughed. "For *one* shot? Arturo...I got three or four shots every day."

"I'm glad I wasn't in that facility; I don't care how strong they made you."

Vlad nodded solemnly. "I am glad you weren't there too." He looked up at the stars, feeling small and happy and invisible. The stars knew nothing about him. "Who do you think is killing our cookers?"

"Someone who's going to regret it." Arturo ground his teeth. "Two cookers in two weeks. Clark pretends it's no big deal, but I know better."

"It was sad seeing Weezer dead. When we would pick up a load, he would always say, 'Hey, Vlad, made any withdrawals from the blood bank lately?'" Vlad shook his head. "I didn't understand the joke, but I liked laughing with him."

"He wasn't making a joke, he was insulting you," said Arturo. "Weezer was a nasty redneck, but he did good work, and I'm going to find who killed him. Find who killed Ellis and Quentin too. Then the joke will be on *them*."

"It didn't feel like an insult. It's hard to tell sometimes."

"This is a new country for you, with a new language. Give yourself time."

"Are you going to tell me again about the value of compound interest?"

"We just have to invest our money *wisely*, carefully, that's all I was saying," said Arturo. "No telecom stocks, no internet incubators...pretty soon we'll be able to tell Clark and his silly wife to kiss our asses. We can retire like kings, go fishing from our own white yacht, with men in uniforms to bait our hooks and bring us orange juice. No more drug addicts. No more crank monsters talking and talking and not saying anything. I want to move to some place where they hang drug users from lamp posts for everyone to see. I have read that in Malaysia...no, Singapore...I think in Singapore they do that. First offense is the last offense. There is no litter on the streets, or drunkenness, and they arrest you for not flushing a public toilet. It is a clean and honest place. That's where I want to go. We could all move there together. Live next door to each other, have dinner together every night. You would be part of my family."

Vlad floated among the stars, drifted in the vast, cold spaces between them. "That's a good dream, Arturo. A *very* good dream."

Dinner with Vlad and *Vlad and Arturo Under the Stars* are "lost" chapters from *THE WAKE UP* (Pantheon, 2004).

THE FAITHFUL WIFE

Indu Sundaresan

The story of a dogged following of convention in an obscure Indian village—a convention that has long been illegal, and has always been cruel.

"Though destitute of virtue, or pleasure seeking else-where, or devoid of good qualities, yet a husband must be constantly worshipped as God by the faithful wife."

—*Manu Smriti* (THE CODE OF MANU) c. 200 BC—300 AD

IT IS THE LETTER that brings him back, because he did not know she could even write. So he comes here to stand in the courtyard, in front of this man who was once so beloved. The letter rests carefully folded in his front shirt pocket, the strap of his camera holding it into his chest. The man seated in the armchair, his grandfather, will never see it. He has not even asked why Ram is here. Tension claws at the air around them, cleaving sharply through their stillness. But outside, in the village that hugs the foothills of small, unnamed hills, all is still quiet.

Morning mist hangs gracefully over Pathra, swallowing the small village in its white folds, swirling between the leaves of the many-armed banyan in the center square. The bullock-cart gutted streets leading in are empty. In a few hours, the square will be noisy with life: village elders sitting in choice spots under the banyan, pedantic with endless cups of *chai*; women gossiping on their way to the vegetable market; urchins chasing stray dogs with a reckless wickedness that comes only in childhood.

Generations have thus used the old banyan, the village square, the vegetable market, why, even ancestors of the pariah dogs. Now though, there is the added blare of film songs on the *chai* shop radio. Yet this is an outward change. Inside, in the people, the village lives in many ways like it did hundreds of years ago.

And that is why Ram is here.

On this cold December morning, as the sun struggles to burn away the mist and announce the arrival of a new day, the square is silent. A cock crows valiantly in the distance, sounding surprised at the lateness of the hour. Within the houses, wives and daughters awake to sweep doorsteps and light *chulas* that will burn well into the night, feeding the day's meals and coffees and *chais*. Later these women will join the throng in the market, shopping bags hung on arms strong from hard work. In the grandfather's house, however, there is no such simple peace for the two men in the inner courtyard.

The man in the chair has seen many years; his hair is whitened by the hand of time, his skin creased by sorrow, and love, and hatred through the years, each stamping its signature forever. The other, in normal times, is impudent with impassioned eyes and a shock of brilliant black hair. Apart in their thoughts, the younger still has the look of the older; his mother was bred of the man in the chair, and she has given to the boy the fire in his eyes, and the chin that stands firm even against his grandfather.

The old man moves finally, his hand striking a match against the grainy wood of his chair. As the match flares in the damp morning air, Ram looks up, lifting a defeated face. His hair falls in an uncombed mass over his forehead. His clothes are crumpled—the suit stained, the previously white shirt no longer a recognizable color, the tie long discarded. Mud cakes his once shiny boots, creeping up the cuffs of his trousers in tendrils of brown.

The journey from the city to Pathra was long. He had caught the last train in just enough time. From the station, there was the bone-jolting bus ride with a driver who sped on the hillside roads aided by a bottle of local *arrack*. Finally, both the old bus and its drunken driver had broken down, leaving the passengers stranded in the cold, dark, raining night. Anger was impossible—this—the passengers clucked to themselves, lifting out their baskets of mangoes, and chickens, and sleeping children, was *karma* after all. Ram let himself out of the bus, swung his satchel and camera over his shoulder, bent his head to the rain and trudged the last weary kilometers to Pathra. Once there, he noiselessly came into this house.

They received him in silence; his grandmother with frightened eyes and an unsmiling face, his grandfather with a mere grunt before leading him to the courtyard. That was a half hour ago. The cup of tea at his grandfather's elbow—none was offered to Ram—has long cooled with an accusing skin of cream. Now they look at each other with the circling awareness of animals in the wild, waiting for a voice to break the silence.

Finally, the old man speaks and out of his mouth comes the age-old vernacular of the village. This matter is too significant for the use of mere English, which both men speak fluently. "Why did you come, Ram? You should have stayed away."

All through the journey he has formulated questions and answers with angry words. But when he speaks, Ram cannot raise his voice against his grandfather, and he replies in the same language, "I could not, Dada. How can anyone stay away from what is to happen here this evening?"

His grandfather glowers from under white, bushy brows. He takes a long drag from his hand-rolled *beedi* and spits out his pre-breakfast *paan* on the dirt floor of the courtyard, leaving a red streak in the mud.

Outside the house, in the main square of the village, the men are gathering with their logs of wood. This is why the letter brings Ram here. He cannot see the men, but now, with the mist still swirling around the courtyard, he hears them. Or rather he hears the definitive thud of one log of wood bouncing off another as the men stack the logs. Somewhere along these hills lies a partially denuded forest which has given its trees so that here in Pathra a human life can be taken.

Ram shivers violently, wrapping arms around his thin chest, his damp clothes clammy against his skin. His resolve is now tougher. He is here because he could not stay away, and he is here because he wants an answer from his Dada.

Ram does nothing in small measures, loves no one in little bits and pieces, speaks his mind as the thoughts come, unedited and raw. But now he is made dumb by a hand he does not recognize. In the cold morning light he stands before a grandfather suddenly turned into a stranger. This man has held him on his knee and talked for long hours. From his words, from his voice, have grown the kings and Gods adorning the walls of Hindu mythology, painted real by Dada's belief and Ram's imagination. From him has even come Ram's name. It is the name of a God exiled by his own father on the behest of a wicked stepmother. It is the name of a God who keeps his faith in that very father— why, even his stepmother—to return triumphant at the end of his exile and claim his kingdom. And thus has

Dada taught Ram to believe implicitly in his elders. And that bright-eyed child Ram, nestled against an aging shoulder, listening to the comfortable rumble in the rheumatic chest, learned to love this man, has learned, or so he thought, to know this man. Today, both that knowledge and his beliefs are shaken. Ram cannot have as much faith as the God whose name he bears.

Last year when Ram came to visit Dada, he spent warm days talking with him, seated leaning against the verandah pillars, watching Dada's face glow as he recounted tales of Ram's childhood. Today, Dada seems suddenly older; his hair whiter, the grooves on his face more pronounced, and in his eyes burns a fervor of righteousness Ram wants to wipe away.

"Your mother was too lenient with you, wretch," the grandfather grates out. "She let you have your way too often. You have to learn that one cannot always have one's way."

Ram flushes. He shifts his weight from one foot to another, wishing his grandfather will bid him sit. It will be unthinkable to do so without Dada's permission, there are some borders Ram can never cross; he has been taught too well. He fills his lungs with a deep cold breath and asks, "Do you condone what is to happen here tonight, Dada?"

As soon as he asks the question he shuts his eyes tight, willing his grandfather to give him the answer he wants, hoping, yet not daring to hope for that answer. Nothing matters at this moment, not the mud caking his shoes, nor the damp misting his hair. The cold, the discomfort, have all gone away awaiting only his Dada's response, to return to plague Ram in less emotional times.

"It is the will of God."

Ram opens his eyes and stares at his grandfather, whose head is bent doggedly to the ground.

"God's will?" he cries, the answer tearing inside him, one border crossed already with that raised voice, "What

God wills you to condemn a twelve year old child to her death for something she is not responsible for?"

"Enough," the old man roars, veins standing out on his scraggly neck. "It is not your place to question a custom that has been passed on from generation to generation for over two thousand years. Who are you, with your westernized customs and morals, living in the city with no contact with the village, to question our way of life?"

"It is against the law, Dada. You know that, the villagers know that. And why is it no one else has heard of the *Sati*? What are you all afraid of? If the police find out, the entire village will be arrested. By keeping quiet about it, all of you—yes, even you—are conspiring to murder a child."

Ram stops abruptly, sensing he has said too much. There is a brief moment, a brief pang when he wishes the words could be taken back, swallowed deep within himself, when he wishes he is that child again on this man's knee, trusting and trusted. But it is too late now. Tied as he is by blood and love to this man, he has to speak.

How can *Sati* be right? Some customs were always wrong, however old they were, this was something *he* had taught Ram. How can it be right for a widow to go to her husband's funeral pyre to immolate herself alive, to go with him where he went even after death? It is too bizarre even to be contemplated. This is a story from history, a past to be forgotten, not relived under the bright harsh gaze of the twenty-first century. This is a story from his myth-history-filled *Amar Chitra Katha* comics, where women jumped off scaffolding into huge bonfires upon their husbands' deaths to avoid capture by invaders. But this is to happen here today, there are no invaders, no marauders, no claimants upon the woman's—little girl's—reputation. Just a vicious need to connect with the past, with a willing scapegoat.

Ram shifts his weight from one foot to another. His

legs cry for the release of rest but his mind will not let him do so yet. He is here in Pathra in quest of a story which fascinates him as a journalist, which horrifies him because it is going to happen with the unconscious blessing of his grandfather. The dead man in question has died a natural death at the age of sixty-three, and less than a year ago he married the twelve year old daughter of a peasant. That in itself is illegal, but shrouded in the safety of an ancient village where people talk little of these things lest their way of life disappear to the will of an incomprehensible urban God, all things are made legal. Now the child, barely into puberty, barely even a woman, is to die in the fire of her husband's funeral pyre just to uphold her family's honor and their prestige. Not to mention, and this is rarely mentioned but mostly taken for granted, the few thousand rupees the old man paid for his child bride.

Ram would never have heard of this but for one incident. The village code, extending strictly even to minor things, was broken by a woman who all her life followed the rules society laid down for her in rigid lines. All her life, until now. When she opened the door for him this morning, in her eyes he had seen fear but also, in that grim glance, defiance.

The news comes to him through his grandmother, a few lines penned in the greatest hurry. It catches him by surprise. Ram has never seen her write or read. Ram has never heard an opinion from her unless it was said to a woman in the family, or to him when he was very young, and so not yet a man. Dadi has always followed the rules. Yet there was the childish scrawl by an unused hand on the scrap of paper tucked into an old envelope. The previous address on top was scratched out and topped with his own. Inside she has not asked him to come—she rarely asks for things—but has simply said, *Beta*, there will be a *Sati* here in two days, the child is only twelve, her husband, whose body lies on a block of ice in his home awaiting the cremation, is the man we talked of when you were last here.

For two hours Ram sits at his desk at the *India Times*, phones ringing on other reporters' desks around him, fans whirring on the whitewashed ceiling. Weighted sheets of paper flutter to the rhythm of the fans. The letter lies spread under his palms. Dadi wants him to come, that much he knows for sure. But why? Is it the journalist she wants or the grandson?

So Ram leaves his desk at the *India Times* and rushes to his village, hoping the *Sati* will not take place and yet, in a sense understanding that it will. As he trudges the last kilometers to Pathra in the rain, Ram knows he will never talk to the woman with gentle eyes who sent him the letter, that she will never admit to it. But as she opens the door, he sees in her spine the strength his mother has, not just from her father who shows it more obviously, but also from her mother who quietly speaks when it is time to be heard.

"This is not murder," says the grandfather, his voice trembling with rage. He cuts sharply into Ram's thoughts with that voice. "She chose the *Sati*."

"*She* chose the *Sati*?" Ram is incredulous. "She is twelve years old. What does she know about *Sati,* or for that matter, anything at all? She is a child, Dada. A baby. A brainwashed little child."

"You can do nothing about the *Sati.*"

"Oh, yes, I can," Ram replies, speaking first always, thinking later. Then he stops. Could he? All through the long night, while the scenery passes by him in flashes of shadows and light, he has thought hard about his decision to come to Pathra. His first instinct as a journalist had been to pick up his camera and race to the railway station. Then, running for the train, on the train, on the bus, on foot in the dark night, he had worried about his intent, his responsibility. Should he simply inform the police and let the *Sati* be stopped? Or should he report the incident, after the fact, in a detached manner? Somewhere, in the back of his mind, a little voice told him that this *Sati* could be stopped, but there would be others, in other villages. Until this one took place, until it was reported in all its horror to the country, people would not choose to condemn it. Ram knows too, that the mere suggestion of a tragedy, is never as powerful as the *fact* of a tragedy.

"Dada," he says in a subdued voice, "Tell me just one thing, do you condone it? If you do, when you die, would you want Dadi to be put in the same situation? Would you want her to be burnt alive on your pyre?"

The old man's eyes stray to the other end of the courtyard where his wife of fifty years is pounding wheat. As the sun, struggling through the mist, sends amber fingers into the yard, chaff swirls around her in golden motes. As if sensing his gaze she looks up from her work and smiles. Both men see that smile, and in that instant, Ram realizes his grandfather knows who has brought him here. Dadi has not spoken to Dada of what she has done, but he has known—and said nothing to her.

"The matter was decided by the village elders and the girl was told about it. To become *Sati* is a great honor, it is the mark of a woman's respect for her husband," the old man speaks slowly, resistance ebbing from his aged body. "It is not a decision of which I approve. I know," he waves away Ram's unsaid words, "I am a member of the *panchayat*, but I did not vote on the matter. I suppose by my silence I assented. But what kind of a life will she have as a widow? With no money, no one to support her?"

"She will at least have a life," Ram says quietly. "That is more valuable than honor, and prestige, and reputation."

"Yes." The old man rolls another *beedi* and lights it carefully, cupping his hands around the flame. "But a mere life is not enough—it is hollow, meaningless, without

173

honor."

"You can say no, Dada."

The grandfather shakes his head. "There are things you do not understand. This child is a widow, marked with sin because of it. She can never marry again. She will have to shave her head, throw off her jewelry, cast away her glass bangles, never wear flowers. She can not laugh out loud, or argue, or play. Her very presence is a blight to her family. She can go nowhere, be part of nothing—no weddings, no celebrations, she will be considered an ill omen."

"This is unfair. Stupid. Ridiculous. No one lives like this anymore, Dada. Does her life not have any value at all? Do her parents not love her? Do they prefer to see her die, and thus, this horrible death?" Ram is shattered. He knows all these rules for Hindu widows, but they are so archaic, so senseless, so unfair. His voice shakes. "Do you believe this to be her fate if she lives beyond her husband?"

And again, there is that silence, until the old man raises his gaze to his grandson's and holds it steadily. "Yes. This is her fate. She cannot change it. This is what she was born to do. If she were my child—I might have done different. But I cannot, will not fight against her parents' decisions. You must accept this, Ram. There are some things we must not battle. Know this, learn from this. This child will die, so that others do not have to."

"How is this even fair, Dada?"

"What will you do about this, Ram?" his grandfather asks. "Will you rage against it? Or will you do something? Write about this. Tell the world; break the silence that hangs over this village. Do what your grandmother wants you to do." He slants his head toward the other end of the courtyard where his wife has stopped pounding the wheat and listens instead to his voice.

Ram sits down on the dirt floor, another border crossed

unbidden, and leans his back against his grandfather's chair. This is what he has wanted—to know that his grandfather is a man with a heart. And this, he realizes, is what Dadi wants too. Even after fifty years she will not ask this question of her husband, she uses her grandson to do so. Ram turns his face away for a moment as his eyes fill. The pain in his chest subsides as though a familiar hand soothes it away, and then comes back again, this time for that child who waits in the village to become a martyr.

Then he turns again to look up at his grandfather and follows his gaze to the woman at the other end of the courtyard. Her pestle thumps against the stone mortar gently, as she has lived her life always, but beneath her strong hands the wheat crinkles and crumbles into powder. In this most important matter, she has molded them both, perhaps she has always done so, and perhaps they—husband and grandson—are who she wants them to be.

Ram turns away again. This will be a small item tucked into the second page of the newspaper, but its importance will grow as time goes by. He will have to get it to the editor as soon as possible, the nearest phone is at the village dry goods merchant, but Ram will not go there. Instead he will walk the five kilometers to the next village, so that anyone who overhears his conversation, albeit in English, will pay small attention. Or so he hopes anyway. He will return to the city unseen. He has to. His Dada and Dadi live in this village.

As the mist finally lifts and the sun bathes the courtyard in its golden embrace, Dada's gnarled hand steals slowly to stroke Ram's head.

STOP PRESS

She walked to the pyre in childlike strides, her glance

unwavering. Away from the crowd. All morning she had waited for this moment in patience as the men stacked logs of wood in the center of the square.

The banyan in one corner stood forlorn, its arms beckoning. But few sat under it. They crowded instead around the men, watching with a horrible fascination as the castle of wood rose, one log interlacing another in a tight embrace. The men worked in grim silence, not once lifting heads to acknowledge the curious bystanders. All day, there was the thump of one log clutching another, building into a grotesque fortress of death for a young child. In the end it piled higher than her, higher than the tallest man in Pathra.

As night fell, a quietness descended upon the square. In an hour, the funeral would take place. But now the square was empty, the stack of logs standing alone as a symbol of what was to come. Passersby did not avert their gaze as they went into the square. The child had been condemned to her death by an entire village. There was no remorse in any face.

Finally, one by one, clad in their best clothes—maroons, pinks, greens and blues, mocking the widow's whites—they crept into the square. Men, women, children, even babes cradled in mothers' arms, all gathered around. Faces gave away little; eyes burned with a fanatical light.

The old shopkeeper's body was brought and laid upon the pyre. Disease had ravaged him long before death came to claim its share. He had been a small man, old and decrepit. It was hard to give him such a large share in history. In this twenty-first century AD, he took with him on his long journey a girl who was old enough to be his wife, but young for everything else life offered.

This is the first reported incident of *Sati* in almost fifty years. The child was merely twelve, but she held herself with a dignity and poise well beyond her years. There was much she did not comprehend, much she wanted to ask, but a fatality, a sort of *karma*, had numbed her mouth.

Clad in the white *sari* of widowhood, devoid of ornaments, her face pale under ebony hair, she walked to the pyre with a look of defiance. Her husband's head was placed on her lap. Her wrists were tied to the logs of wood. Only then did her brave look falter. But it was too late. Her forty year old stepson walked thrice around the pyre with a flaming torch before lighting the fire. As the flames licked their way greedily upwards, the girl twitched and pulled at the ropes which held her.

The crowd began chanting '*Sati Ma*', their voices rising to a crescendo, their hands folded in prayer to the girl who would forever be revered in their village as the epitome of wifehood. The girl screamed as the fire roared towards her. It devoured her clothes, her hair, the ropes had burnt through... She rose for a brief moment, a living inferno, then collapsed in a heap as the fire engulfed her still form.

Sati has been illegal in India since 1829. Yet more than a hundred years later, the entire village of Pathra condemned a child to her death to uphold a dubious custom. There was no regret at the end of it. As horrible as it sounds, they all wished they had done it before. But where would they have found another child willing to listen to her elders thus? Willing to give up her life because she was obedient? The *Sati* was conducted in the greatest of secrecy. This reporter watched hidden behind the shutters of a house in the village square.

After the fire died down and the frenetic crowd had disappeared, the girl's family went home, their heads held high, their expressions of deep pride. Today their daughter had done what no other woman had done for a long time, even in Pathra. Tomorrow, they will build a shrine for their daughter in their house. People will come from neighboring villages for a glimpse at the garland-bedecked photograph of their child, and will pay for the privilege.

The parents had already sold their daughter once to the highest bidder—the sixty year old man who married their child. Now, they have sold her again.

WRITING ABOUT WRITING

The Case for the Arts and Humanities

We begin with the body, our instrument.
We begin with the limbs and torso of a dancer,
the cadenced breath, the voice of a poet,
the eye and dextrous hand of a painter,
the sculptor's skin against sculptor's clay,
the ear where melody and harmony play.
Our long discourse is corporeal, be it
of philosophy or society, law or the psyche,
events physical or metaphysical.
We know by how a thing smells, we learn
by sweet and sour, by rough and smooth,
by every common sense, and by heart, too,
and by brain, that soft-tough muscle,
wherein we seek those truths beyond our Age.
While warships move slowly and world events
sway our conscience and pain our hearts,
let us think what we shall leave to entropy.
We who use the world must revisit it.
Let our works, like our words, express in time
the truth of our nature, for good or bad,
for the jury is out and the foreman has asked
for a fully detailed, illuminated transcript.

— *Marvin Bell*

FACING DOWN THE MONSTER

Terry Brooks

EVERY TIME I sit down to write, I am afraid. This is the time, I think, when I will have nothing to say. Or if I have something to say, it will not be anything worth reading. I am afraid my words will be ordinary and uninteresting, my images stale and familiar, and my story trite and predictable. I am afraid I will discover that I have lost the magic of storytelling that has served me so well.

I understand the source of this fear. It derives from the expectations of my publisher that the book at hand will sell more copies than any I have written before. It derives from the expectations of my readers, who have come to believe over the years that I will not publish anything that doesn't represent my best work. It derives from my own expectations that I am a competent writer, workmanlike and consistent, able to assure myself that I can do what is needed each time out.

I have been writing stories for more than fifty years, starting when I was ten years old and continuing to the present. There has never been a time when I wasn't writing fiction of some sort. In the beginning, it was mostly bad fiction—a lot of fits and starts, trial and error, and thrashing around in a thicket of confusion over what I wanted to or could do. It took me the better part of fifteen years to finally settle on a story that felt right. It was a tough slog reaching that point. But during that time, I was never afraid. I had no reason to be afraid. My expectations were small and they were exclusively my own. No one was waiting for my Magnum Opus. No one thought I would produce the Great American Novel. Especially me. I was just trying to write something decent. I might have been confused, but I wasn't afraid.

The confusion ended with the publication of *Sword of Shannara* when, at the age of thirty-three, I could at last tell myself that I had a sense of what was needed to write a book. But confusion was replaced almost immediately by fear. Could I do it again? What if my confidence in knowing what was needed was misplaced? What if I had just been lucky the first time? What if, having traveled the trail once, I could not find it a second time? I had written one book that was publishable, but there was no guarantee that I would be able to write a second. I didn't want to be a one-book wonder. I wanted to be a writer for the rest of my life. I understood the odds against making this happen, and it had everything to do with consistency. What if consistency were like water and mine the hands it would spill through?

I have stayed afraid ever since. After twenty-five books, it is no longer a rational fear. I know this; I tell myself I don't need to be afraid anymore. But I am. The fear starts with the writing of the first sentence of each new book and peaks at just about the same time and place along the way—halfway through. At that point, I realize in shock and dismay that I have written exactly the sort of book I was always afraid I would write. I have written a book so bad that it will make even my editor laugh when she reads it. I have concocted a story that lacks passion or power. I have created a monster.

You should understand that this monster is not the monster of full-blown writer's block, although the two are related. I am still able to write, after all. What I am unable to do is to convince myself that what I am writing has any value. If I press ahead, it will be the equivalent of driving off a cliff. My fear is not of being unable to write; it is of writing poorly.

I have learned to walk away from it. I am panicked, but I know the drill. I leave my monster where it is, shut down the computer and find something else to occupy my time, something that takes me out of the house and away from my work. I do not come back to my monster the next day or even the next. I do not come back for at least several days and not until I feel ready to face it down. The power of the monster is not to be underestimated. It is my own power, created by me, born of my fear of failure. Such monsters have broken writers before, and while I do not feel that this one will break me, I cannot be sure.

When I sit down to read anew all of what I have written earlier, a ritual by now after so many years, I am armored in a sense of expectation. I have regrouped, and I know that my monster will not be as terrible as it first seemed. My expectation is shaped by my determination not to be overpowered. I am a writer, and writers must come to terms with monsters of all sorts. It is in the nature of what they do that most of these monsters will prove to be less daunting than they seem. This is particularly true of monsters born of fear; they seem much more ferocious than they really are.

So it goes each time. The result of my rereading is universally satisfying. The writing is never as bad as I believed. This is not to say that it is always good. Almost always, there are mistakes in execution. There are inconsistencies. There are wrong turns and forgotten plot threads. But the story is not the disaster I believed. The monster only made it seem so in a moment of weakness that was mostly of my own making. The monster is good at duplicity. It is a chameleon with many faces. It whispers of lies and half-truths. It tests my resolve.

I cannot explain why I must do battle with it each time out other than to suggest that doing so is a part of the writing process. What matters is that much good comes of our confrontation. The monster keeps me honest. I am a seeker of truths about the human condition, as are all writers of fiction, but such truths are not uncovered easily and are not always recognizable for what they are. The monster shields them in the same way that parents will shield small children from strangers. A stranger must first provide credentials and establish intent if a friendship is to be initiated; writers must do the same if truths are to be revealed. It is a form of testing, a trial by character.

Reassurance and confidence surface quickly once the writing resumes. When the monster is confronted, it begins to diminish almost immediately. Fear gives way to determination; my writer's journey is underway once more, and the hoped-for truths begin to reveal themselves. Momentum builds, and the fear recedes into the background as the shape of the book becomes clear. It does not dissipate entirely; I will not let it. At least the threat of its return is necessary if I am to keep my focus. But it is no longer a monster of unmanageable size; it no longer threatens by its mere presence. It is a ghost of things gone past.

I wish I could explain this to the writers I encounter in my classes, at schools, and during conventions and conferences, the writers who are struggling with their own fears and uncertainties. I wish I could reassure them that fear of failing is a good thing, that their monsters are as necessary to assuring their adherence to the craft of writing as is my own. But the monsters formed of our fears take different shapes and manifest themselves in different ways.

They are peculiar to each of us, attack us uniquely, and require us to banish them in our own ways.

Writing requires courage, a confidence of self that allows us to believe that we have something important and interesting to say. It is hard to believe in ourselves in the beginning because we have no reliable way to measure the value of what we have done. That task is for others, for our readers, and until we reach those readers we mostly have only ourselves to turn to. But even after being published, we are never entirely sure—not if we are honest. Writing is a form of magic. It is a genie in a bottle that we have been fortunate enough to release. But there is nothing to guarantee that the genie will give us more than a single wish.

A little fear keeps us from assuming that we are incapable of mistakes. It keeps us honest with our work, keeps us focused on our efforts to write well. We mustn't turn away from our fear when it surfaces in the course of our writing. We must take it in our arms and embrace it. It is there to help us.

BORN TO WRITE?

Elizabeth George

DURING A RECENT teaching appearance at a writers'
retreat, I overheard two of the writing instructors in
conversation following a morning presentation. "If I hear
one more word about outlining, I'm going to scream," was
the remark that stood out for me. I found this comment
interesting, for in some ways it seemed to illustrate the
divide that tends to exist between what I'll call the born
writer and the developed writer.

Oddly enough since the situation couldn't have been
less Shakespearean, thinking about those overheard words
led me to consider the trick played upon Malvolio in *Twelfth
Night*, that prank arising from the forged love letter from
Olivia in which she reassures her manservant in a spurious
declaration of devotion to him that "some are born great,
some achieve greatness, and some have greatness thrust
upon them." In the way that thoughts tend to germinate
one from another, I peregrinated from Olivia's "love letter'
to a paraphrasing of Shakespeare that ended up as "some
are born writing, some achieve writing, and some have
writing thrust upon them."

Those who are born writing are the blessed natural storytellers. They are individuals who have a gift for language, a talent for turning phrases, and a passion to move onto paper all the stories that dwell in their heads. They talk about having ideas "just bursting to get out", and they write naturally and almost mysteriously. Make no mistake about it, though: For them, writing is not a simple process. It's not without trial and error, without thought, without multiple drafts. Yet it *still* seems to emerge from their minds in a mysterious fashion, inexplicable even to them and as a consequence largely unteachable to anyone else. They find it tough to explain *how* they do what they do. They just know that they are blessed with being able to do it.

Those who achieve writing, on the other hand, learn early to love language, reading, and story. They putter away at short stories and poems; they even try their hand at the novel. They have talent, but it needs developing and so they must find a way to develop it. Some use the trial and error method, writing story after story and novel after novel until they finally get it right. Some take creative writing classes or enroll in MFA programs. Others read books on writing while still others attend retreats and conferences in which various aspects of creative writing are explored. What these individuals are intent upon doing is getting a toolbox and loading it up with implements of the craft. They know that there is no simple cookbook out there, filled with easy-to-follow recipes for everything from crime to children's fiction. But they are the types who like to go into situations fully informed, and they find that classes, books, or retreats help them do this when it comes to creative writing.

Then there are those who have writing thrust upon them. They are the individuals who write at knife point, and every English teacher who's ever lived has encountered them in the classroom. They only write when they absolutely have to, and for them it is akin to being placed upon the rack when they must produce so much as a paragraph. This group I will dismiss with that description, for it is the other two groups who concern me just now.

For the natural writer (and for that you can read the born writer), creating poetry and prose is an innate process. For the developed writer (and for that you can read the achieved writer) it is a nurtured process. And the compact we have with our Creator is that no one gets to decide which group she is going to be born into. It's just how the cards were dealt; it's just how things are.

Additionally, what we don't get to decide is whether we are literary or commercial writers. What we write— along with the *way* we write it—also is an example of just how it is. Our writing reflects the way we see the world. It represents our vision and how we translate our vision into language.

Still, the common thread for *every* writer is something called process. Every writer has one, whether she is able to articulate it easily (as most achieved writers can and do) or not (as many born writers can't and don't), and the job facing every neophyte writer is to discover what her process is. But first she must identify herself as someone who was born writing or who needs to achieve writing. If she was born writing, her process will likely develop over time as stories emerge from her brain. If she is going to achieve writing, she will learn and develop based on a growing understanding of the tools of the craft.

But ultimately, each writer's process is an individual one, not identical to anyone else's. It comes from picking and choosing: either picking and choosing from the trial-and-error method of the born writer or picking and choosing from the exposure that the achieved writer has had to writing books, classes, and programs. During this time of developing a process, though, the neophyte writer— born or achieved—must try this and that in a course of discovery, looking for techniques that will dispel darkness, illuminate character, and open story.

At the end of the day, there is no writer on earth who can *ever* tell a neophyte writer what will work for her anymore than someone can tell that same writer what to do to solve her life's problems. Advice can be given; experiences can be recounted. The journey, the discoveries, and the decisions, however, are ultimately up to the individual.

So if I were to give advice to people who want desperately to write, this is what I would tell them:

First, most people have committees in their heads, keeping them from writing what they want to write. This committee comprises individuals from childhood: parents, teachers, siblings, scout leaders, ministers, etc., and the committee generally engages in discouraging comments and disheartening putdowns. If you are one of these people and have a committee stopping you from putting words to paper and completing a project, you must first identify the members of your committee and you must dismiss them. Thank them for sharing and tell them goodbye. Affirm yourself—hourly if necessary—and recognize that, because you are an adult, *no* committee from your past can defeat you without your participating.

Second, some people have dreams of writing best sellers and becoming instant millionaires. To them, I say: become realistic. The majority of people who love to write do not ever get published. They write because writing is who they are. The majority of the people who get published do not become millionaires. If you want into this game for big money, you're better off blowing your wad in Las Vegas. At least you'll have bright lights, big city, and free drinks around you while you do it.

Third, some people write the same novel over and over in an attempt to "get it right." If that describes you, stop doing this. Go on to the next novel. Then write the *next* one. Remember that no one improves by creating the same piece of art again and again.

Finally, a few people are looking for the magic bullet, the key, the secret pill, the looking glass or anything else out there to make this an easy calling. To you, I say, wise is the person who gets real, gets into acceptance, learns who she is, and gets to work.

You do not get to choose the ease—of lack thereof—of your process any more than you get to choose your talent. Nor do you get to choose the type of writer you were born to be. What you do get to do, however, is to learn who you are. Throughout the journey of burgeoning craft, you get to experience what exactly it is that comprises your talent and your passion. You get to choose how to use what you've been given.

And believe me, there is blessing in that.

BRIDGET'S KITCHEN

Mark Lindquist

"WHAT ARE you making?"

"A frittata."

"How do you spell that?"

"F–r–i–t–t–a–t–a."

"What exactly is a frittata? Remind me."

"An Italian omelette, a cross between an omelette and a quiche."

"Cool." I'm at the kitchen island typing on my laptop, writing a very short story.

Bridget says a frittata is the perfect way to start a Sunday and she's beautiful and so I take her word on things like this.

Bridget's kitchen is open and airy with a butcher block island in the middle, cast iron pans hanging from the ceiling, and a French door opening to the shaded patio.

This is what's called a country kitchen, I think.

Bridget's bustling about, assembling pans and bowls and ingredients on the tile counter bordering an old-fashioned white Wedgwood stove with steel trim. She's wearing an off-white peasant dress that would be see-through if not for the flowered apron that covers from her breasts to her knees.

195

I'm almost forty and don't know how to cook.

"Should I put on some music?" I offer.

"Okay."

"What's good music for cooking? Nirvana?"

"No."

"Pearl Jam?"

"No."

After a long pause I say, "Leonard Cohen?"

"The Beatles." Bridget says. "How about 'Rubber Soul?'"

When we met, Bridget told me she was 32, but later she admitted she was 34.

I skip "Drive My Car," start with "Norwegian Wood." There are speakers in the main room and in Bridget's kitchen.

"*I once had a girl…*"

"So," I say, returning to my place in front of the laptop on the island, "how exactly do you make a frittata?"

"Well, first you sauté onions and garlic," Bridget says, picking up an onion. "Then, when the onions and garlic are ready, you add spinach and sun-dried tomatoes. "

"Got it," I say, nodding as I type.

"Are you listening?"

"Of course."

"Two eggs per person," Bridget continues as she cuts the onion—chop, chop, chop—like a total pro. "After the olive oil, you grate some cheese. I'm using Monterey Jack. Add the cheese on top of the omelette. You can also add fresh basil leaves. Then you let it cook. Takes about twenty minutes."

"Got it."

"That's it."

"Quick lesson."

"I hope someday you do something with what you've learned," Bridget says as she finishes chopping.

"Well," I say, "someday, something."

THE KETTLE BOILS –
OUT POURS A NOVEL

Bharti Kirchner

M.F.K. FISHER, the eminent food writer, was once asked why she wrote about food and not about love or war. She is said to have replied, "Because I'm hungry."

Hunger was one of the primary reasons why, as an erstwhile cookbook author, I once spent hours in the kitchen devising new recipes. Surrounded by an array of ingredients—from elegant stalks of leek and pearl-like grains of rice to ruby red cherries and bittersweet chocolate—I would let my imagination run free, chopping ingredients, grinding spices, and choosing cooking techniques. Part of the process also involved taking elaborate notes: What size skillet? How much cinnamon? When to lower the heat? My hunger would be partly satisfied from seeing the colors and shapes, sniffing the aromas, and listening to the musical clinking of the spatula on my pan.

Finally the dishes would be ready. One particular meal consisted of braised leeks, coconut-infused vegetable curry, rice, and cherry-chocolate tart. Tasters—family and friends—converged on my dining room where I happily served them the results of my latest frenzy of inspiration.

One day that all changed. I was in the kitchen chopping garlic or perhaps beating eggs—I don't remember exactly—when an image flashed into my head. A girl of seven dressed in fine clothes and jewelry stood by a camel in the deserts of western India. Darkness was descending. The honey-colored horizon foretold a sandstorm was coming.

Who is she? Why is she there in such weather? Where might she be going?

Later, sitting in my study, still puzzling over the image, I came up with a pair of sentences: "Seven, her people had always believed, was an auspicious number. One's life began anew every seven years."

And so I began, playfully at first, composing the story of Meena Kumari, a village girl betrothed to her favorite playmate. In her milieu, mass weddings of children were common, although the bride and the groom would not live together for many years. On the night of her wedding, bandits swooped in from the desert and kidnapped her, fatally injuring her mother in the process.

I stopped writing there and showed the pages to a friend. What happens next? she inquired.

I didn't have a clue. It was as if a bigger story was out there somewhere, as if I was getting the whiff of smoke from a fire burning in the distance. I kept on writing to find out, my hours in the kitchen by now greatly reduced.

Expressions of concern came from well-meaning friends, family members, and readers: How can you throw away your kitchen skills? How can you deprive us of your recipes? Shouldn't you just stick with what you know? Aren't novels and cookbooks at opposite ends of the rainbow?

I couldn't answer them. I could only keep imagining

subsequent events in the life of Meena Kumari, and put them down on paper. Now, many years later, after publishing that novel, *Shiva Dancing*, and several others, I am finally ready to address the issues that were raised.

Novels as a genre deal with all aspects of the human condition rather than a specific activity, such as cooking. As a writer I find story-crafting a bigger challenge than recipe-crafting. In the expanse of a novel, a writer's entire being comes into play. Her moods, desires, and experiences somehow find expression through the characters, plots, and situations. The story takes its form and its wings from the writer's life energy. When the work is complete, the creation flies away, quite unconcerned about the creator who gave it birth and now lies on the ground, bruised and exhausted.

Why on earth, then, did I leave the warmth of my kitchen and venture into this torturous territory? The answer, I believe, is hunger of a different sort than that mentioned by M.F.K. Fisher, a hunger for something less tangible, a hunger for a larger vision.

At the start, the story doesn't reveal itself fully. It teases the fringes of the writer's consciousness, then flits away, leaving behind a trail of clues—the gesture of a character, the flash of an event, a stream of emotions. The writer tries to make sense out of these tantalizing fragments. Hunger to experience, to own this other universe, propels her forward. The path isn't always clear.

Have I, then, thrown away those fragrant hours in the kitchen to chase and romance some imaginary wild beast? Quite the contrary. My earlier experience pays off. Food insinuates itself into my novels. It does so innocently as a metaphor for nurturing, a connection to reality, but also imbues a scene with an extra punch and meaning.

In my second novel, *Sharmila's Book*, my American heroine arrives at the house of her prospective in-laws in New Delhi. She is baffled by the cool reception she receives, until such time as she is served a frothy glass of *lassi*. It is no ordinary glass of *lassi*. The servant, instead of simply blending yogurt, ice cubes, and sugar, has lovingly added specks of toasted mustard seeds as a pungent counterpoint to the sweetness; he has taken a liking to her. Over time these two disparate characters form a liaison, born of a feeling expressed by those tiny black mustard seeds. Then as she searches for clues to the tragic death of a family member which she believes will illuminate the mysteries of this household to her, she encounters a scheme of silence. The servant is the one to reveal the truth.

So much for the plot, one might say. What about characters, the crucial element of a story?

I always start a new novel with the good intention of doing a detailed background chart on each important player—height, weight, age, occupation, that sort of thing. In truth I have never actually completed one. The story grabs me by the collar and demands that I get down to the nitty-gritty of putting pen to paper: Do the work it dictates, not the work about the work.

And so, I take a short cut and simply find out a few salient points about my characters. What do they fear? What makes them happy? Who do they love? How does food and beverage contribute to their roles in the story, if they do at all?

Here's an example from my third novel *Darjeeling*. It is the story of a family who owns a tea plantation in the Himalayan town of the same name. In keeping with Indian custom, the eldest daughter, who also happens to be more responsible and more popular than her younger sister, will some day inherit the prosperous tea estate. The only catch is this: Although she takes her morning cup of tea out of habit, she isn't particularly enamored of the beverage. Nor is she interested in the agricultural and commercial aspects of the commodity. On the other hand, her rebellious younger sister is a connoisseur of fine tea, devours trade journals on the subject, and practically lives in the tea fields. A cup of tea means much more to her than a pleasant drink she takes in the morning. Even so, the tradition-bound family doesn't consider her as a candidate.

Through many twists and turns, the story leads to an answer of the question: Which of the two women will inherit the tea estate at the death of their grandmother? Put in other words, will passion triumph over tradition?

With my fourth novel *Pastries*, I went one step further. I set the story in a warm friendly bakery filled with aromas of apple, cocoa, vanilla, and almonds. The protagonist, a talented young pastry chef who owns the bakery, lives for the sake of baking. As the novel begins, this pastry maestro confronted with many challenges in career and life finds herself losing her baking skills. Whenever she tries to make her best-selling Sunya Cake, something goes wrong. She burns the chocolate, her cakes collapse, and she even forgets to add the sugar. The question that arises is this: When you lose the ability to do what you love the most; how do you get back your skills and your life?

Eventually my heroine conceives an elegant solution to break through her baker's block.

Right now, I am back to my writing desk pondering my next novel, attempting to decipher the motivations of yet another character tormented by difficult circumstances.

When my well-meaning friends, family, and readers ask me for recipes, I say: I can no longer give you the exact measurement of spices, the right skillet to use, the precise time it takes to cook the ingredients.

I can only show you a sliver of someone's life, a few

heightened moments, some joys and trials garnished with an insight or two.

I can serve you a story.

EMERGING WRITERS

Rule of Thumb

My thumb's naked profile
Reminds me of Napoleon —
Bulging belly
Arrogant arch of back.
At half the height
He rules all the hand
A monarch separating me
From my ape-ancestors.

Today my potentate —
Ambushed between door and jamb —
Forces me to my knees
Makes me plead for mercy
A peasant in the presence
Of His Majesty
The Digitator.

— *Fred Melton*

Among the Shadows

She will eventually get the disease.

But he knows it's the other way around—the disease already has her
As she hovers in their curtained kitchen like a marionette, dazed
Suspended between the refrigerator's hum and the clicking of the clock.

He steps to her side, slips his wedded hand into hers
Strokes the hair he's nuzzled a thousand and three times
Whispers, *I'm right here, I'm right here*, to break the spell and draw her
Back into their fragile and fading lives

As the Alzheimer's retreats, then crouches
Among the shadows.

— Fred Melton

HOLLENBECK'S
FIRST RULE OF MEDICINE

Phyllis A.M. Hollenbeck, MD

Humor and candor, experience of heart and mind, and craft:
Doctor Hollenbeck's Ten Rules of Medicine.
This excerpted work of eye-opening nonfiction is her First Rule.

BEING HUMAN
"My God, my God, how soon wouldst thou have me go to the physician, and how far wouldst thou have me go with the physician?"

—*John Donne,* "DEVOTIONS," 1623

I GIMPED ALONG on the knee for six weeks. I am a fifty-three year old woman, a physician for twenty-six years, and I do not like doctors. Most of them, anyway. The two nicest sentences that have been said to me in my career are "You don't look like a doctor," and "You don't act like a doctor." I always take them as compliments at cocktail parties.

I like being a patient even less. The role of the patient means being infantilized, or worse, blown off by a guy, usually, in a white coat whose training was essentially an enforced adolescence. He goes to medical school as a nerd and when he gets those magic initials after his name he becomes an eligible bachelor who still has no inter-human skills. Too many of these presumed geniuses should have done something else to make their parents proud.

My left leg limp bothered my office mate, a good guy doctor, even more than it pained me. Tom is a man who writes plays and connects with his patients; as a pseudo-patient I was a definite challenge. After numerous days of watching me pull myself out of my desk chair and wince, he reached the apogee of his annoyance.

"What the hell did you do?"

"Nothing. I sat cross-legged for forty-five minutes writing on my laptop and I had a little twinge when I unkinked my leg. It hasn't been the same since."

"What are you doing about it?"

"It's better with the knee strap and the anti-inflammatory samples we have."

Tom made a face like I do when I ask someone "How much do you smoke?" and they say "Not much."

"You need to see an orthopedist. You've probably got a torn cartilage and it isn't going to sew itself back together."

This I knew and I also knew that if weeks of what we call "conservative management" by a family physician (myself) hadn't gotten the swelling down or extinguished the searing pancake of pain right through the center of the knee that I enjoyed every time I put direct weight on it, I needed one of those surgical subspecialists to take a look.

"I'll just give it another couple of days," I said.

Tom looked as relentless as sin, even though his brother is the priest. "No—even if you can stand it much longer I can't. You know you need an MRI and then an arthroscopy so somebody can go in and trim the damn thing."

I limped in and out of exam rooms four more times and came back to my desk to dictate. I felt the laser-guided spite of God boring down on me as soon as Tom walked back into our office.

"I don't want to see a jerk", I said.

"I know a good orthopod; he worked on my knee."

"You're still wearing a brace."

"I'm five years older than you are and so are my joints and I could barely walk until he cleaned out my knee."

"How old is he? I don't want a boy doctor who looks like some student I've taught."

"He's got gray hair."

I rubbed my knee. "Does he know how to talk?" I asked.

"Yes. He's Irish. You'll like him—or you can come back and poison me."

The next afternoon on my day off I was standing at the check-in opening in a wall on the other side of which sat a young woman. "I'm Dr. Hollenbeck," I said, "and I'm here to see Dr. O'Neill."

"Let me look it up." Her computer screen scrolled. "We have you seeing Dr. Harkins."

"No. My medical assistant made the appointment yesterday from our office and I know who I'm supposed to see. Dr. Palmero, whom I work with, specifically referred me to Dr. O'Neill." I smiled.

"Well, I don't know who Dr. Palmero is. And Dr. O'Neill is all booked up. You'll have to see Dr. Harkins. He's really good with feet and ankles, and it's for your ankle."

"No. It's my knee."

"Well, you can reschedule."

"No I can't. It hurts too much and I only have Fridays off and you have no idea how much it took to get me in here. And I know who I'm scheduled with."

We were at a healthcare stand-off.

"Well, you'll have to see Dr. Harkins first and then I'm sure you can see Dr. O'Neill another time."

I smiled. As my dentist says, smiling at people like this is what breaks crowns. "I'm sure after I see Dr. Harkins that I'll want Dr. O'Neill to take a look at my knee before I leave."

She stared at me. The cursor blinked more naturally than she did. "You have to fill these papers out."

I limped to a seat in the waiting room, quickly filled out all the forms on the clipboard (thank God I know the drill), and limped back up to the slot in the wall. Fifteen minutes go by and Ms. Receptionist calls my name and tells me I have to "go through that door to billing." More slow ambulation but at least when I am on the other side the two young women there smile when I walk in; maybe it's because they collect the money.

I look at the billing slip and it says "Dr. Harkins." I tell them about the appointment mix-up and no offense to Dr. Harkins but I'm happy to wait to be worked in (and that I'll add Dr. O'Neill onto my schedule if he ever has to be seen for acute bronchitis), and one of them says "Oh. I'm really sorry to hear about the mix-up. Let me see what I can do."

Ten minutes later she spooks me while I'm reading back in Ms. Receptionist's domain because she quietly crouches down next to my seat and says, "You're all set."

The woman who finally takes me back calls out only my first name as she guards the door to the royal chambers. She says "the doctor will be right in" which I know is a lie but I sit up on the table swinging my legs and looking out at the roof of the hospital. I memorize the newspaper I have with me. Dr. O'Neill eventually comes in; he introduces himself and smiles.

"Thank you for working me in."

"No problem—I like taking care of people."

Ahah—a live one.

He pushes and pokes and I say it hurts right there and he says "you need an MRI and if it confirms you have a torn meniscus you'll need arthroscopy sooner rather than later. If you want your knee back."

I do. He has to help me off the table and as I limp out of the exam room he says, "You can't wait another day to have this done."

Out in the hall Dr. O'Neill introduces me to Dr. Harkins who is immobile. He looks like he was sure I was a real estate agent and never a doctor and his eventual handshake has less animation than those lifelike robots at Disney World. My mother would watch his manners and say *"Who brought you up?"* I mentally thank Tom and the billing woman for saving me from the fate of being stuck with him.

In the course of my career in medicine I have decided it is not the gender of the doctor that counts but the degree of jerkdom. If it's tricky for me to find a physician whose brain crackles with the thrill of science and can also make a patient comfortable enough to be able to tell their story, imagine how hard it is for the average human being. Some people in the profession should not be there. *Who lets these people in?* Like clones like, so limited beings on medical school admissions committees pick their own kind because a candidate who uses both sides of their brain scares them and highlights their own shortcomings. And it is primarily men who decide who makes the cut—across the country women do not often run medical schools, academic or clinical departments. I know this firsthand having been "the first" or "the only" woman more times than I can stomach, and from the stories of colleagues. Even men who combine art and science as physicians are often discriminated against; at a 250-physician group practice where I was the head of the family practice department, the guy whom I would have picked for my family was disparaged by the medical director as "not tough enough". This chief was someone who did not learn everything he was supposed to in kindergarten.

Medicine is a *service* profession. I believe this idea causes chest pain in many of my colleagues. The practice of medicine is a sacred trust, and my heroes in it are Renaissance people—intimately acquainted with the arts and scientific knowledge; who know that "history is ninety percent of the diagnosis;" that if you listen to the patient they will tell you what is wrong with them (this doesn't mean that someone will waltz into your office and say "I have a pheochromocytoma"); who taught me to "take a history the way the famous Willie Sutton robbed banks— because that's where the money is." They are clinicians who understand that if by the end of taking a history you have no idea what diagnostic bin the patient's complaints belong to, you're sunk; and that often when you open the exam room door you're facing a stranger, someone like all of us who does not want to be isolated in pain or fear.

It's "show time" when you cross that threshold and what you have to show is that you give a damn. Your first job is latching onto the telling phrase from the patient because those words light the way to using your medical wits—not quickly scribbling a prescription, or the acronym "MRI". I remind medical students that you can only do a physical on a human in a few variations, as rarely does someone with dextrocardia arrive so you can listen to their heart sounds over the right side of the chest; but histories come in infinite forms. Over a hundred years ago the giants of this profession described many diseases (and yes, these illnesses are named after these dead white guys, but deservedly so), by using their brains to meticulously connect stories and then the laying on of hands.

The definition of a good doctor is not "he's great at (1) cutting into you; (2) putting a tube up one of your orifices or into the arteries that feed your heart muscle; (3) treating your kidney failure"—that is just "a pretty good doctor." The great ones are out there. They read your face when you're in front of them and not just your EKGs.

Medicine still operates like a priesthood. Let me turn this on its ear—now that women are allowed to go to medical school the calling needs more "Sister Doctors" with the power to change the culture, and male and female inductees who emulate them (including their usually much more legible handwriting). Life has thrill and challenges and pain and undeserved suffering and that is what patients carry with them—they need caring as well as any possible cure.

No specific religion is required to believe in both the intangible as well as the technical and to be the conduit of that to a fellow human being. The education I sought out and found, my longing to learn, my need to always observe and understand—and serve—have given me guiding "Rules of Medicine" that have stood me in good stead throughout my career. They are tenets that all those who aspire to this profession should know and never forget; that all students of medicine must live by. And anyone who has ever been a patient, or loved someone who has been one, or will be a patient, must understand these rules; for we are all "students of medicine" at some point in our lives.

RULE # 1

THEY'RE CALLED VITAL SIGNS FOR A REASON

Dr. Main stood by my desk and handed me a piece of paper. "I saw this lady today, and I ordered a CT scan and some lab tests—you might hear about her on call tonight."

I smiled at him. Stephen Main was known for leaving

each day before the stroke of five, so I considered saying nice of you to stay and risk turning into a pumpkin, but I behaved myself.

"What's her story?"

"She's forty-seven, new patient, I don't have any old records." He shifted his weight. "Five days of lower abdominal pain."

I scanned the faxed CT report: "...large transpelvic mass, ill-defined—abdominal and pelvic ultrasound to be done to further delineate its characteristics." I clocked my eyes back at him.

"What about her exam?"

"Not anything specific—but her abdomen was a little tight."

"Like an acute abdomen?" We both knew that meant a surgical emergency.

"No—just kind of hard." He swallowed. "I did a pelvic exam, but I couldn't find the cervix."

I let that hang in the air; I didn't ask him why he hadn't just come down the hall and asked me for help, especially since I did most of the women's care in our clinic. But I thought it.

Instead, I looked him over. "So what do you think?" I asked.

He didn't say a word.

I found Dr. Main's medical assistant and asked for Olivia Simpson's chart.

"How did this lady look, Tammy?"

She addressed the floor. "Not very good."

I scanned the place in the chart where the vital signs are written. No pulse recorded, only a solitary blood pressure—of eighty over fifty.

"Did you do posturals?" I asked.

"No, I...I don't know what you mean."

I explained to her that checking blood pressure and pulse in lying, sitting and standing positions could mean everything because of the information they carried. I told her not to feel bad about this and only silently wondered why Dr. Main hadn't taught her to use this tool.

The beeper went off with a call from Louise in the laboratory.

"Yes, doctor, I have a critical result."

"Let me guess; on Olivia Simpson."

"Bingo."

Olivia Simpson's white count was three times normal with a shift, which meant her immune system was sending in the type of white cells who act as the Marines and go in first to fight an infection; but her red blood cell count was only one third of what it should be. So I knew she'd been bleeding before today—or still.

"Is the patient there, Louise?"

"No, doctor—Dr. Main's order didn't say anything about that. But I have her phone number."

I got the voicemail voice. Fifteen minutes later Dr. Roberts paged me from radiology.

"I've got Olivia Simpson's ultrasound results," he said. "Hard to identify each part of the mass but her uterus is about twenty centimeters and it's full of pus or blood, or both." Now the white cells were mobilizing like a mob and swimming in a thick red sea, inside a womb swollen like a pregnancy halfway to completion. But this was no baby; it showed only an ugly face.

"Do you know where the patient is?"

"No—but you could call out front to the check-in area. She was here with her husband."

They weren't there now. I alerted the triage nurse in the emergency room in case Mr. and Mrs. Simpson rolled in; I was afraid they were too polite and would sit quietly in the waiting room until her name was called. I tried the emergency contact number in the chart—busy four times.

Twenty minutes later the x-ray technician called me. Olivia Simpson and her husband had come back to the radiology department because they weren't sure what Dr. Main had wanted them to do.

"How do you feel, Mrs. Simpson?" I asked over the phone.

"Okay." She gave me permission to speak with her husband.

"How does she look to you?"

"Well, she was in a lot more pain several hours ago." *When she was in the office.* "But I think she's a little better now."

"She doesn't complain much, does she, sir."

"No. She hasn't been to the doctor since the birth of our child."

I told them what I knew and why I didn't want her to go home, and then I called the ER to let them know the patient and her husband were on their way downstairs.

Two hours later the telephone rang at home. It was Dr. Foster in the emergency room.

"I have Olivia Simpson here. I rechecked her red blood count and it's a little higher."

"That's because she's too sick to drink any fluids and getting dehydrated."

"She wants to go home."

"What's her blood pressure?"

"About eighty over fifty. But she's a small woman."

"Not that small; that's child size. She needs to be admitted."

"There aren't any beds."

"Look. Pus—blood. Neither of them are good and we have no reason to think that either one of them have stopped. Call gynecology and have them put her on their service."

I hung up and went to bed secure in the belief that Olivia Simpson was where she belonged.

At twelve-thirty the next day our secretary, Elizabeth, stood at my office door.

"Dr. Hollenbeck, that lady you were so worried about from last night is on the phone; she says the pain is a lot worse."

"She's calling from the hospital?"

"No, she's at home. Her husband's with her."

I thought as I breathed in. "Tell them to get right in here."

Olivia Simpson somehow walked in, supported on the arm of her husband, with their teenage daughter crying as she trailed them into the exam room. The patient's blood pressure lying down was eighty over fifty with a pulse of 110 beats per minute, the edge of the high normal range even though in that position her heart didn't need to strain against gravity to aim enough blood to her brain to stay conscious; when she sat up, her pressure slid to seventy over forty and her pulse jumped to 162 beats a minute. I didn't try to stand her up again.

I nodded to my nurse whose hand had been on the phone to call 911 as soon as I had eyeballed the patient and had a few numbers to communicate. As two intravenous lines, oxygen and the EMTs went in, I asked her husband what had happened in the emergency room the night before.

"They told us to call for an appointment with the gynecologist this morning." He handed me a piece of paper—the discharge instructions from the ER. A computer generated printout proclaiming a diagnosis of "abdominal pain," no closer to her precise, stealth danger than where he and his wife had started twenty-four hours before. "When I called this doctor's office today they told me she couldn't be seen until next week."

I reassured Mrs. Simpson's daughter that her mother wasn't going to die even though I knew that with the delay in care she was now one day closer to it. At the emergency room her mother spiked a temperature of 103 degrees Fahrenheit, was given three liters of intravenous fluids and four liters of "crystalloid" (a liquid precisely designed to keep her blood vessels open), and transfused with two units of blood.

This time a different ER doctor asked the OB-GYN on call to come in; he presented the patient's status over the phone and this new specialist pronounced the patient "too sick to stay at our facility." *Well—now she was.* Mrs. Simpson was transferred directly to the intensive care unit of the nearby university hospital; the next morning, as soon as she was stable enough, the doctors there drained almost a liter of pus, enough to fill a big plastic jug of soda, from her uterus. She "made it," surviving this perfect storm of destruction, only because she was just forty-seven and otherwise healthy until it hit her.

What went wrong? How did this "near-miss" happen? The picture was present from the beginning, but the doctor who saw this patient first didn't look.

In my work I care closely for my patients and am ever vigilant for the one who could slip through my hands. The practice of medicine is that serious, and you never know when *that* person will walk in. This isn't always easy, or possible, and it can't always be finished in one encounter—but it is the prize on which to keep your eyes. It means wanting to stretch your mind around what doctors call the "chief complaint," the patient's ticket of admission to your office; and stopping for that moment, to hear that sound in one's heart and mind, can make all the difference. For that bell that clangs back and forth between need and response is one that tolls for each of us in this existence, before the one that John Donne wrote peals at the time of our death. It is the sound of hoping to stay connected to life.

Mrs. Simpson had a blood pressure of eighty over fifty, a number transparently lower than normal; she admitted to pain. A few simple questions would have elicited that she was stoic and probably downplaying her symptoms, but asking about her old records and finding out there weren't any would have confirmed just how much, i.e., how much pain and fear, it took to get her to come to a doctor. But even before all that, by checking her blood pressure and pulse in lying, sitting, and standing positions, just how ill she was would have been written in neon. Even if this lady was unwilling to admit to dizziness, or being "sick," her numbers would have shouted it out.

Why didn't the first doctor to "see" the patient use all his wired organs to gather in all this information? It is the disconnection between knowledge and sense.

Caring. That's it. It is the penultimate vital sign, without which the others are useless. You sit in the exam room with a doctor and your unspoken words are "*Help Me.*" Tell me that everything is all right—whether I'm here for a yearly physical or a check-up for my heart, my diabetes— my cancer. If something is not right, tell me what we can do. Help me tell you that the masked worry over my strained marriage is what's "eating at me," and needs one treatment, while the crater it's burnt in the lining of my gut is visible and needs another. And when there is nothing more "medical" to do, tell me how to face that; and don't leave me. Don't leave me alone.

The cleavage starts when the doctor doesn't *care*. All of us as physicians are human and so any one of us, on any given day, can be tired or distracted or angry but below all that must course that abiding caring that pulls you back to why you are in that room with a patient.

This job requires a person of restless passion, diving into science as they swim towards a fellow human being in need. Someone who likes problems: preventing, understanding, and solving them. Someone who gets a thrill and has an eternal fascination with figuring people out—both their human bodies and their human minds. I do not believe that drive can be taught; it can only be honed and polished. It must be there in the beginning in the person chosen for that seat in medical school. As none of us has a direct line to God a physician cannot always make a difference; but wanting to know, deeply, the mechanisms of health and disease and of being human, and not slapping that knowledge aside can make all the difference we can.

This is a cautionary tale. You see what you want to see. Dr. Main "sees" someone every ten minutes; up to forty people a day. But you can quickly assess someone, as they do under more stress in emergency rooms, if you look first for what's vital.

Several weeks after Mrs. Simpson, a woman sitting in one of my exam rooms related the story of her mother's recent trek through healthcare. She finished her story, looked at me and said:

"To be a patient these days you have to pray."

Amen.

F-150

One hundred and sixty-thousand gallons per minute
surge under a pink plastic ball
twelve inches in diameter,
hollow and buoyant, bobbing playfully
against the tug of a quarter inch stainless steel tether
tied to the bumper of a nineteen eighty-four
Ford F-150 long bed pick-up
caught, for the moment, between the ancient mud
and timeless rock forty-five feet below.

The river that took the driver
from behind the steering wheel
holds him in the channel somewhere further down,
near the trailer ramp at Hydro Park
where it's cold and dark and still.
His flesh feeds the younger fish
in the shallows where the spawn
grow strong enough to fight the force
that powers the turbines further north.

It's nearing spring, the lower snow is melting,
always toward the river's flow
and on and on where oceans roll,
some say where life began.

— *Daniel Sconce*

Sleeping Apples

The frozen sky, gray and dense,
passive and heavy with unfallen snow,

once chilled Pacific mist,
full of promise and rivering east,

now drawn down into forest rows
of sleeping apples,

the memory of fruit still in their boughs
where a single bird is singing,

the fallen fruit her audience,
a leafless tree her stage.

Her solitary song is sung
to no one,

but sprinkled, like seeds,
for a harvest yet to come.

— *Daniel Sconce*

THE YOKE

Stephen John Walker

*A soldier serving in Berlin tells of a chance meeting between a man
from the modern world and a woman from another age.
He is reminded of how much we take for granted,
what we may have lost, and that we are all
at the mercy of the forces of nature.*

NIKKO WAS SNORING. Again. Not the rhythmic
snoring of someone in deep, comfortable sleep at home
in his own bed, but sporadic grunts, snorts, and wheezes
of a fitful sleep sitting up in the driver's seat of a truck.
That is where we were, sitting in the cab of his Volvo
eighteen-wheeler waiting for the storm to pass.

We had pulled off the highway to Moscow into a Russian
village when the whiteout conditions of the blizzard made
driving too dangerous. It wasn't much of a village—one narrow
snow-covered street running between single-story unpainted
houses. Icicles hung like rows of daggers from the overhanging
roofs partially hiding the scalloped wood borders under the
eaves and around the shuttered windows—the only attempt
at decoration on the log or rough-hewn bare exteriors.

The padlocked shutters, hung on heavy iron hinges, gave the impression of vacancy, but from two of the houses light escaped through cracks in the wood.

Nikko had parked his tractor-trailer under the single street lamp in the village square. Its weak yellow light shone on the front of an old Orthodox church, now the headquarters of the local Communist student organization. Large colorful posters showing Soviet youth in heroic poses adorned the outer walls on either side of the ornately carved padlocked doors. In the center of the square was a fountain. Not really a fountain, just a concrete trough circling a platform with three statues: a soldier holding aloft a flag in one hand and a rifle in the other, a man with a large hammer, and a woman with a scythe. The water in the trough was frozen and covered with snow. Sheets of ice flowed down the sides of the trough and into the street.

What a lousy place to spend Christmas Eve, I thought as I wiped the moisture from the inside of the window on my side of the truck's cab. Even the heater wasn't able to keep them from fogging up. Riding shotgun on a load of building materials for our new embassy was not exactly what I expected to be doing as a Foreign Service officer with some very basic Russian language training. My special passport made this Volvo tractor-trailer a massive diplomatic pouch, off-limits to Soviet police and KGB agents. There would be no "bugs" in these bricks. The trailer's sealed rear doors had to be checked frequently, and as I opened the door of the cab the blast of cold air woke Nikko.

"*Pérkele!*" he swore in Finnish. Shaking his head and straightening up in his seat, he reached for the pack of cigarettes on the dashboard. A cloud of smoke hit me in the face when I climbed back into the cab. It seemed like the storm was letting up a little.

"Storm over," Nikko said. He had rolled down his window to let out some of the smoke. "We can go now?"

I nodded and he turned on the defroster and windshield

wipers.

"*Pérkele!*" Nikko swore again as he turned on the truck's headlights. A short heavy-set woman was standing in the middle of the street. The sudden light must have startled and blinded her. She stopped for a moment before continuing toward the square, her face turned away from the glare of the headlights.

Head and face wrapped in a scarf, she wore a heavy, brown, military-style coat, a gray mid-calf length skirt, and high-topped black boots. Across her shoulders lay a wooden yoke with a bucket hanging from each end. One bucket looked like it was made of dark wood or leather, the other of metal.

She walked slowly to the side of the fountain, stopped, turned around, and bent forward to lower the yoke and buckets down to the snow-covered ground. Facing the fountain again, she put a gloved hand into a coat pocket and pulled out a hammer.

"We go now?" Nikko asked.

"No," I said. "Wait."

With several slow, deliberate blows the woman broke the ice in the trough. After carefully returning the hammer to her pocket, she picked up the leather bucket, submerged it in the water, and then placed it on the rim of the trough. She did the same with the metal bucket, but placed it on the trough's rim some distance from the other. With her back to the fountain she bent down, picked up the yoke, placed it on her shoulders, and then sat on the edge of the trough between the two buckets. She inserted the ends of the yoke through the handles of the buckets, took two deep breaths, and stood up. Her first step, on fresh snow, was short and hesitant. The next was on a patch of ice. She slipped and fell.

I climbed down from the cab of the truck and walked quickly, but carefully, to where she lay. On her back she still grasped the yoke with both hands. The buckets hadn't tipped over. She was breathing rapidly and her eyes were open.

"*Zdrástvuyte, bábushka,*" I said in my rudimentary Russian. "Are you all right? Let me help you."

The scarf had fallen off and I could see that she was very old: her face a mass of deep lines and creases. Ice crystals stuck to the facial hair around a toothless mouth.

"The water—the buckets—did they spill?"

"No. They are still full," I said reaching down to help her to her feet. "Are you injured?"

"No. The ice—I was careless."

I was surprised how light she seemed as I lifted her. From the bulk of the clothing, I thought she would have been heavier.

"When you are ready I will help you lift the buckets."

"You are not Russian?" It was more of a statement than a question.

"No, *bábushka.* American."

I bent over and brushed snow off the yoke. Along its entire length and on all sides were the faint outlines of carvings. Looking closer I could see that they were hunting scenes: deer, bear, wild boar, spear-armed men on horseback with packs of dogs, but also, near the ends, churches and saints. Worn nearly smooth by decades of use, it had once been a thing of beauty. Lifting the heavy load I rested it on her shoulders.

"Thank you. I am a careless old woman."

"What is that called in Russian?" I asked, pointing to the yoke.

"*Igo,*" she answered. Then, after a pause, "Don't you have them in America?"

"No. Not anymore."

She took a few short steps, stopped, and turned toward me.

"But—how do you carry water?"

STAY

Anna Sheehan

"Stay" is a dark whirlwind of a teen's desperate life.
The reader is drawn into the mind of a victim,
whose pain and isolation have touched the heart of another.
Finally revealed is the source of her suffering, all the while
struggling with dissociation and social enigmas.

MY ROOM IS, of course, filled to the ceiling with clutter and incongruities. Andy stares at it all. Like my bag, filled with every necessity of life, tampons and underwear and socks and cosmetics. My room has everything else. A hot pot and food stand on my dresser drawer, my clothes, all from the Salvation Army, are on the floor. The clothing my mother bought me, that's all in drawers or even still in the pile of bags against the wall. I never wear what my parents buy me. I'm trying to be as self-sufficient as I can be, I don't like taking anything from anybody. I make most of my own meals here in my room.

Andy looks out of place.

I shrug.

"This is your room?"

I nod. I never talk much. When I do it's choppy, strong. I will be strong. I must be strong. Quiet, but strong.

Andy's like that too. Weight lifter, wrestler, high school jock, popular.

What on earth is he doing here with me?

But one time he saw me. For once, he finally saw me. Me, in the background, watching him. Watching his strength. He wasn't with his sport friends, the popular jocks who are known all over the school. His parents weren't watching him, and he wasn't all filled with adrenaline and his eyes blinkered onto a goal. When he's not with them he can sometimes see for himself, and he saw me. I wasn't like everyone else, I didn't demand things of him. Win for the team, take me out, give me pieces of yourself, even when you don't know what that is. I accepted him. We accepted each other.

Then we kissed. He's not like he seems, he's not like he looks, he's not like I thought him when I first saw him. He's strong and fast and powerful outside, but he's weak and scared inside. His father dominates him. I sympathize.

He looks around him, stunned at my posters. I don't care what they depict, I pick them up at Goodwill and put them on my walls to cover the blank white staring, so that nothing can see me. Kittens and rock stars and evil demons. They overlap and overlap. They even cover the ceiling. My windows are curtained. It's like my hair, dark and died black and long and shaggy, and the thick black mascara I hide behind.

He takes off his sweatshirt, his school varsity sweatshirt. The tank top underneath bulges with his musculature, round pectorals and arms like Adonis. I love his body. He does too. Not how it looks, he's indifferent to that, but he loves how he feels inside it. Not like me. I can't stand being trapped inside my body. I keep wishing I knew how to escape it that didn't involve death. Or drugs. I've never taken drugs, they scare me too. Everything scares me. Even Andy sometimes.

He sees me watching him, and our eyes catch. He's only in jeans and a tank top; I am covered in three to six layers of black Salvation Army clothes, always. But we are alone, and he knows I have a body.

"Maybe we should go back to the living room," Andy suggests.

He sounds scared. I know he's hinting at my mother, who has just cleared the table of her delicious supper, which Andy ate with gusto. He's always hungry, he's always growing. Mother didn't see Andy. She didn't see me. She rarely sees anything but herself, but she will be the dutiful housewife. She will cook the meals and clean the home and wait for her husband to come home from work, and she will obey her husband. She will. Daddy doesn't notice her. I wish he didn't notice me.

"Mom won't notice," I say, falling onto my unmade bed. "She never notices."

This is the first time he's come over. I don't go over to his house anymore. His parents don't like me. They think I'm dangerous. Maybe I am.

Andy spins in a slow circle, looking at my room. He's never seen any place like it. I stare up at him from the bed, where I am lying, my head at the foot, on the wadded up blankets. He turns his face to me. I blink at him. There are times he's like a startled deer, or a wild animal. He seems like a wild animal in my room. Like a wild mountain lion on the transway on the highway. Lost like that. I smile at him.

He looks around, he looks around again, at the piles

of newspapers in the corner, the boxes of books, the heaps of faded black clothing. The light is fading and my shades are closed anyway, so it's very dim, and the door is closed, and it's almost night. He seems more and more uncomfortable. I don't know what to say.

It seems he can stand it no longer. He approaches the bed and stares at me in the fading light. "What do you want me to do?" he asks me. Lost. Confused. Uncertain. We've never made love.

I only blink at him, and I see him tense like he does when I blink at him slowly. He says I look so beautiful, with those haunted eyes. That's the word he used, haunted eyes.

"What do you want?" he asks again, sitting down and peering at me.

Like I want him to kiss me, or take me up in his arms, or make love to me. Like I know what I want.

"Tell me what you want," he says again.

Isn't that always his problem? Aren't his parents always telling him what to do, and doesn't he always listen? He's closer to me now, whispering almost in my face, and we can both feel the kiss surfacing like a breaching whale, but he still needs me to tell him. Why does he need me to tell him? I can't tell him anything. I can't tell him what I really want. "I want you to think for yourself," I tell him.

He tenses again, and he looks so beautiful himself when he does that, the tendons flexing momentarily in that powerful neck. We are already close. He leans forward and kisses me, finally.

I feel drowsy, I think he does too, and this is my bedroom, intimate. He lays down beside me, and I don't mind his weight next to me. It is marvelous, in fact. I can't stand that I like it, and I bury my face in his chest, like I do sometimes, when I hate that I love him. Hiding from myself, hiding from him, in him.

"Oh, what is it?" he asks me. He's always asking me that. I think I look hunted. I can never tell him. Never tell him.

"Hold me," I whisper. I don't know if he can hear me.

He holds me. He holds me like I'm about to be taken from him, in a grip like a drowning seaman, but I love it, and I grip him back.

If only I could always feel this way. Feel so safe. If only I could stay here forever. If he would stay. His arms are strong and his chest is strong and he holds me tightly and I feel so safe. I don't care if this won't last, I don't care, it's so nice now.

We rest. Perhaps we sleep. It is so peaceful, so wonderful, such a miracle to lie here, me safe in his arms. If only, if only, if only.

I remember last week. He hadn't introduced me to his friends much. I didn't want to meet them.

"Do you wanna go to the party tonight?" he asked.

I didn't know. I'd never been to a party before. "Okay," I said quietly.

He picks me up. Using his father's car. For once, I am beautiful, for him. For once my eyes aren't hidden. For once my hair is back. For once I wear a lighter dress, only two layers. For once, for once, I let people see me. I look normal. I'm afraid.

The house he drove me to is larger than mine. It's filled with people. Music I've never heard before and don't understand pounds through the rooms. People flow through the rooms like blood through veins. The house is alive. I don't want to be eaten by it, but Andy is used to it, and draws me into the mouth of the beast.

People stare at me. They've never seen me before.

They ask Andy who I am. They ask in a way which suggests that I have no business being there. It wasn't my idea, don't ask me.

Food I don't like is spread on a table. Pizza and pretzels and things I've never eaten. I dip corn chips in my soda and nibble on those. Andy seems on edge. There is a role he has to play here, strong, unified, a social animal, a pack animal, part of the herd.

The herd has never accepted me. I was kept away from them for so long by the time I ever got near it, I was already an outsider.

He talks loudly. I can see he is distancing himself from me. I expected no less.

I shrink to a corner. I wish I had my mascara. I wish I was wearing black. I wish I had something to hide behind. I let my hair down and let it hang over my face. I look down. I'm not sure I can be here—too many bodies. Too many souls behind too many eyes. Andy is across the room, then out of the room, and I am alone.

The two beside me are chatting about some upcoming party, and why X broke up with Y, and what's going on in the latest episode of some situation comedy. I want to scream at them, think for yourselves! See what's really happening! Talk about something important! I never speak unless it matters. Instead I get annoyed and glare at them and their shallow lives. They stare at me. "What's up with her?" they ask each other.

The same thing that's always up with me, but I don't tell them that. I stare at them and they go away.

My ears are hurting, and I feel like I'm in a meat grinder, the press of so many bodies around me. I can't breathe. I keep my back to the wall and try to leave my body.

Andy realizes I'm not at his side, and comes to find me. Such a gentleman. "Hey, you all right?" he asks.

His voice is quiet again, silky again, like a lioness purring to her cubs. Not a lion. The male will eat the cubs. Munch their heads right off. I saw it on the nature channel. Males do that sort of thing. Andy's come back to me.

I want to say, Yes, I'm fine, let's dance, or something like the rest of the kids are doing, but all I can do is press closer to him, my arms at my side. He's like a coat to protect me from the cold chill of all these hot bodies pressing around me, smothering me. His arm goes around me, instinctually. He looks torn. This is a party. Parties are what he's supposed to go to, to be sociable at, to be part of the crowd. It's where the girl always wants to go anyway.

"You wanna get out of here?" he asks me finally.

I only stare at him. My eyes are hunted, I know.

"Come on," he says, and pulls me away from the wall, through the morass of humanity and out into the quiet and the cool night air. I breathe a sigh of relief. I can breathe again. Not so many people. I feel safe again. I don't say anything.

"I'm sorry," he says. He still seems torn. The idea of oppression doesn't make sense to him. He's so used to it. "I should have realized," he says. His head is down.

I press my head into his side and he takes off his letter jacket and wraps it around my shoulders. He's always giving me his jacket. I always look cold, even when I'm not. I'm always hiding.

We walk for a long time. I have no business ruining his social life. I, who have never had one. We do not always talk. He finds it soothing, that I do not demand words from him, or anything else. But now the silence is comfortless. "I'm sorry," I say. I pull away from him and give him back his jacket.

"What's the matter?" he says.

I go over to a street lamp and lean against it, staring into the road, still shiny from the earlier rain. What can I say? How can I tell him, I'm no good for him? I'm damaged goods. I know this. He doesn't. Yet. "I know you'd like to try," I say, "but I can't live in your world."

He sighs, his muscular shoulders hunched. He slips his jacket back on and jams his hands into his pockets. There is a long silence. His parents think I'm strange. His friends think I'm scary-weird. I find his world oppressive.

Finally he breaks the silence. "You wanna go away, is that what you're saying?" he asks. "Are we over?"

I close my eyes. "No." I didn't mean to say it. I don't want him to go.

He takes a single step toward me. I don't look at him, but I can see him anyway. "Maybe I could try to live in your world," he says.

I shake my head. "I don't have a world." I feel this is true.

He still seems torn. The part of him raised by his father and following that herd of horses in there wants to say, fine, go, I never liked you anyway, you're too weird, everyone tells me to leave you. I think the inside of him wants only me. "Can I visit your nothing then?"

I laugh. It was funny. I love him so much. I nod.

His shoulders sag with a mixture of relief and confusion. "This isn't going to be easy, is it?"

Nothing ever is. "No."

He stares at me with eyes wide and innocent. "What are we?" he finally asks.

I look up, directly at him.

"Am I your boyfriend?"

Boyfriend? What's that? What's that supposed to mean? I shrug. It is my only answer. Like I have any friends, boy or otherwise. Like I ever did. Except now I have Andy.

"Is that a yes?" he asks.

I shrug again, and look back to the wet road, shining in the streetlight.

He reaches out to touch my cheek. Unlike with everyone else, I don't turn away. His touch doesn't burn. "Does that mean you're gonna stay?"

I look up at him. "Yeah," I whisper, very slowly. "I'll stay."

He rouses himself when the moon rises through my curtains. "I should go home," he says. His parents are waiting for him, I know. His father, his mother, they care where he is at night. They ground him for things like this.

"Stay," I say. It is quiet, but desperate. I can't explain it. Do I want him to see? No, no, no, I don't ever want anyone to see. But I don't want him to go. I *don't* want him to go. A litany starts in my mind, No, no, don't go, *stay, stay, stay, stay, stay....*

"But..." He hesitates. Direct order. He always has trouble disobeying direct orders. I have the same problem, though not with words.

"Stay," I say again, plead again. "Please stay."

He stares out the window, those beautiful blue eyes worried, confused. He can see it's important. He weighs his decisions. They'll ground him, or punish him. Somehow they'll punish him. They might punish him already, it's already pretty late. "Okay," he says. His arm tightens around me.

I close my eyes again. He'll stay. I sigh, and breathe in his scent, heady, sweaty scent, clean and powerful, powerful. I controlled this wild beast, I kept this powerful creature, and he stays because he wants to. *I love you,* I say without even whispering. Only my lips against his neck, his shoulder. *I love you.* He doesn't know what I'm saying, but his arm tightens again. His strong, powerful fighting arm.

We sleep again. I hear music from a passing car. My mother goes to bed, but I hardly notice. She doesn't check in on me.

I can tell he's hungry, he's always hungry, but he doesn't make any move to get up and neither do I. This is too comfortable, too much of a miracle. This stolen season, only grown-ups get to feel this. This quiet night peace. Not sixteen year olds. Not kids like us. He makes no dishonorable suggestions. He's too much of a gentleman for that. I don't know what I'd do if he did. I couldn't. Couldn't. It would be too awful. But I like to think it's okay if you love someone. Most of me is too scared.

His hand strokes my hair. Does he love me? It seems like it. Doesn't matter. He's here now. I feel safe. I feel *safe.*

But I'm not safe. I'm never safe. The car pulls into the driveway. I cringe. I know. I knew. Did I plan this? No. I don't care. He can't be here. I shouldn't have let him be here! He can't... "Get up!" I whisper.

"What?" he says, confused, dazed, half asleep.

"Get up!" I hiss.

"Why?" he asks.

I don't tell him. "Get up," I hiss again. "Get out." Of the bed, I mean.

"Jesus," he mutters, looking on the dark floor for his shoes.

"No," I say. He looks up at me. I don't know what I'm saying. He clearly doesn't understand. "Hide?" I plead.

"Why?" he asks again.

"Hide!" I hiss. I grab his shoulders and guide him to the closet. The closet has no door. It never did. It

lies in shadow, however. Darkness. Unseen. "Stay here!"
I command.

He sighs and looks at me like I've gone mad. I have
gone mad. I feel mad. I never felt sane, but I feel mad.
I want to kiss him, I want him to comfort me, because I
know what's coming next. But I can't kiss him. I can't
touch him. I can't think about what's coming next.

I go back to bed. I can see him, my eyes night-
sighted. He stands in the shadows. He glares at me.
His glare burns. He thinks I'm being strange again.
Doesn't he know yet why I'm strange? No. No. He
can't see me, really. Or can he? I love him. He does
love me. He loves me. He'd have left before when I
was strange, if he didn't love me. We've been together a
month, and he hasn't left yet. Despite his parents, despite
his friends who think I'm weird, and who I won't bow
down to like he does, despite all that. He loves me. If
only as teenagers can love, if only just beneath the surface,
he loves me.

I'm thinking these thoughts to distract me from the
sound of my father in the living room, who has opened
the door, who has taken off his jacket, who has hung it
in the front hall, who has opened the refrigerator. Late
night worker. Comes home at midnight. Mother knows
when he comes. She doesn't care.

I see lights under my closed door. I see Andy slide
down the door jam to the floor of my closet, his head
shaking. My eyes are wide open, my eyes are fixed on
him. He gazes back at me, and then looks away, looks at
the floor, confused. My stare is too deep, but I can't
help it.

My father has had his midnight snack, mother always
leaves it in the fridge for him, mother loves him so much,
mother cannot see.

The lights go off in the kitchen, they grow brighter,
the hall light is on, father is coming to bed.

I close my eyes to block off the sight of Andy, so I can't see him in the closet, can't see his expression as my door opens, as light spills across me, lying in bed, wide awake. I always wake up when daddy comes home. Daddy expects it.

Daddy stands, silhouetted in my bedroom door. He enters, he lifts up the covers, he makes no notice of the fact that I'm still in my clothes. I often sleep fully clothed. I have often ever since—I lie still. I always lie still. There is no difference about tonight, except the pair of eyes, watching, the feral eyes I told to stay.

Daddy is busy, as usual, his long, coarse hands unzipping his pants, reaching for my underwear, getting ready to press me down with his weight, his horrible cologne scent. This happens most nights. Daddy.

I lie still when the explosion comes. Did I know it would come? Did I expect it to? Of course I did, but no, I didn't. I sit bolt upright. Andy has left the closet, and is roaring like the wild animal I know he is, my father is against the wall, and Andy hits him, and hits him, and hits him. He hits him until I see blood on my white sheets, until the horrible cologne smell is buried in scent of Andy's righteous sweat, and the sound of fists hitting my father's skull, the scent of blood. His power is amazing, it fills the room, I breathe it, the wild animal is unleashed, or leashed to me, and daddy is battered by its ferocity.

I watch. Am I sad? No. I'm not happy. I feel no triumph or glee in Andy punishing my father. I feel no grief for my father who is now still, and Andy still beats him, and he is still still. Andy snarls, grabs his shirt, knocks him against the wall, once, twice, picks him up in those powerful arms, and against the wall again, his breath panting, his face enraged, confused. His wrestler's muscles strained in a fury they aren't used to feeling. No competition, no sportsmanship, only this wrath, this sudden understanding, this sudden explosion of rage. A feeling, a real feeling, like I realize he has never felt before.

Andy stops pummeling my father, and pants, and swallows, and are his eyes moist? He sags onto my father's chest with a sound like a sob, like the sobs I sigh after father leaves the room. Andy turns to me.

I am still. I am still. My eyes are wide open, and Andy stares at me. He's so confused, he's so frightened, I am still. I am calm.

"This is why you wanted me to stay," he breathes.

I only blink. There are no words. My eyes do not linger on my father, but on Andy's tortured, wild, feral face. Andy. My love. My wild horse. My savior?

He finds me against the headboard and wraps those powerful arms around me, those arms which may have just crushed the life out of my father, those arms which make me feel so safe. I feel safe again. I close my eyes and he rubs his hand, sticky, through my hair. Sticky. Blood. There is blood on his hands, like the blood on the sheets when father first came to my room. Andy is shaking. I am still.

He kneels between me and the broken rag doll which is my father. He guards against the view of it. He protects me from him still.

My mother has awoken. My mother is at the door, is going into hysterics at my door, runs to my father, insists to him that he's all right, that he's breathing, that she's going to call the ambulance, that everything is going to be okay. She kneels hysterically at father's side and I can't see her, I can only hear her, but she won't shut up. She does not berate Andy. She does not berate me. She does not actually see either of us, only father.

I see only Andy, I smell only his healthy strong scent, feel only his arms around me, his shaking body, and he sees only me. Or whatever is inside his closed eyes.

Mother finally leaves the room, and Andy looks back

at my father, who is breathing. Who isn't dead. I don't know how I feel about that. I honestly don't care either way. Or I can't care. Andy stands up, then comes back to me, and then stands up, and I cling to him suddenly. I don't care what happens, but no, Andy is not to go away. No. He pulls me from the bed and I fall to the floor at first. I have forgotten how to walk.

Andy grabs my school bag, my bag with everything in it, the bag I have kept with me since I entered high school, my bag with socks and underwear and tampons and aspirin and books and everything I ever need. My bag, my security, and his sweatshirt and his shoes, and my shoes and slips them into my bag, and we leave my mother's house.

On the curb he helps me on with my shoes and he slips on his own sneakers and he puts his sweatshirt over my shoulders and as the police and ambulance pull up the street, before they can see us, he takes me away from the flashing lights and away from my mother's house and away.

I grip Andy's arm. Andy is muttering something, curses, oaths, anger, at him, not at me, sympathy, for me, passionate misery for me, why didn't you tell me?

"I did," I say, as I realize that I did. As I realize that I saved myself. "I said stay."

ABOUT THE WRITERS

ABOUT THE WRITERS

Kathleen Alcalá is the author of a short story collection, *Mrs. Vargas and the Dead Naturalist* (Calyx), and three novels set in 19th Century Mexico: *Spirits of the Ordinary, The Flower in the Skull,* and *Treasures in Heaven.* She has received the Pacific Northwest Booksellers Award, the Governor's Writers Award, the Western States Book Award for Fiction, and the Washington State Book Award. She is a co-founder of, and contributing editor to, *The Raven Chronicles*, a magazine of multicultural art, literature and the spoken word, and has been a writer in residence at Seattle University, Richard Hugo House, and most recently a visiting lecturer at the University of New Mexico. A long-standing member of Los Norteños, a group of Latino writers in Western Washington, Kathleen has published fiction and nonfiction in numerous magazines. She lives on Bainbridge Island, Washington, with her husband and son.

Peter Bacho, a Tacoma, Washington, based author, was the Distinguished Northwest Writer in Residence at Seattle University (Winter 2005). He is the author of five books. His awards include an American Book Award for his novel, *CEBU*, The Murray Morgan Prize, and a Washington Governor's Writers Award for his collection of short stories, *Dark Blue Suit*. His newest novel, *Entrys*, will be published next year by the University of Hawaii Press.

Marvin Bell delivered the PNWA 2000 Conference keynote speech. His seventeen books of poems and essays include *Rampant* (2004) from Copper Canyon Press and *Poetry for a Midsummer's Night* (74th Street Productions). He recently retired from the University of Iowa Writers' Workshop after forty years on its faculty. His poem, "The Case for the Arts and Humanities," included here was written while serving as Iowa's first Poet Laureate. He and his wife Dorothy live half the year in Port Townsend, Washington.

Terry Brooks was born in Sterling, Illinois, in 1944. He received his undergraduate degree from Hamilton College, where he majored in English Literature, and his graduate degree from the School of Law at Washington & Lee University. A writer since the age of ten, he published his first novel, *The Sword of Shannara*, in 1977. It became the first work of fantasy ever to appear on the *New York Times* Trade Paperback Bestseller List, where it remained for over five months. He has written twenty-one novels, two movie adaptations, and a memoir on his writing life. He has sold over twenty million copies of his books and is published worldwide. He lives with his wife Judine in the Pacific Northwest and Hawaii.

Stella Cameron is the *New York Times/USA Today/ Washington Post/Booklist* best selling, award-winning author of sixty historical and contemporary novels and novellas. She has won the *Romantic Times* Career Achievement Award for Romantic Suspense and the *Romantic Times* Best Romantic Suspense of the Year Award. She has been a RITA finalist, and is the recipient of the Pacific Northwest Writers Association Achievement Award for distinguished professional achievement enhancing the stature of the Northwest literary community. Stella and her husband live in Seattle, Washington. They are the parents of three children.

Meg Chittenden has published over a hundred short stories and articles, and thirty-five books in various genres, in the thirty-four years this nationally-acclaimed author has been writing. These include three books for children, romance novels, paranormal fiction, and mystery novels. Many of her books have appeared on bestseller lists. Her recent publications include *The Charlie Plato Mystery Series*, and *How to Write YOUR Novel*, and most recently, *More Than You Know*, and *Snap Shot*, both suspense novels published by Berkley. Meg is a recipient of the Pacific Northwest Writers Achievement Award, an Anthony Award for "best short story," and an "Otter" for *More Than You Know*, from the Left Coast Crime Convention.

Robert Ferrigno was born in Florida, growing up on the last paved street of a small town, spending his youth cutting secret passages through the palmetto thickets with a machete and occasionally burning down those palmettos for the simple pleasure of seeing the trucks arrive, sirens blaring. After graduating with a degree in philosophy and a Masters in Creative Writing, he moved into a high crime area of Seattle and started playing poker full time. Five years later he got restless and used his winnings to start a punk rock magazine, which led to a gig at a legit newspaper in Southern California. Over the next seven years he flew with the Blue Angels, drove Ferraris and went for desert survival training with gun nuts. Great job, but he wanted to write novels.

Elizabeth George is the author of thirteen crime novels, a book of short stories, and a book on fiction writing. She is the winner of the Anthony and the Agatha Awards for best first novel, France's Grand Prix de Littérature Policière, and Germany's MIMI. Her novels are sold internationally in more than thirty languages, and eleven have been filmed for television by England's BBC, and are regularly shown on PBS's *Mystery!* She is a committed teacher, having acted as an instructor across the United States and in Canada. She divides her time between her London flat and her home in Huntington Beach California, has a condominium in Seattle, Washington, and is in the midst of building a home on Whidbey Island, Washington. She is married with no children, although she will confess to being owned by two very adorable miniature dachshunds call Titch and Lucy.

Phyllis A.M. Hollenbeck, MD, is a native of Boston, and received both her undergraduate and graduate medical degrees from Brown University. She chose Family Medicine as her specialty, seeing it as the one from which all excellent care flows; it also means taking care of people, in the words of Dickens, from "the lying-in to the laying-out." Her career has encompassed solo practice, academic teaching, and administrative leadership. She knew she wanted to be a writer before deciding to be a physician, living through words all her life, (including in music and mothering), penning long and short fiction, nonfiction and poetry.

J. A. Jance is the author of thirty mysteries, one volume of poetry, and two children's books. Refused admittance to the Creative Writing Program at the University of Arizona, she, like many other successful writers, came to writing through a back door opened for her by the Pacific Northwest Writers Conference. Born in South Dakota and raised in Arizona, she's a former teacher, school librarian, and insurance salesman who didn't start writing her first novel until age thirty-nine when she was a single mother with two little kids, no child support, and a full time job selling life insurance. She wrote her first three books between the hours of four a.m. and seven a.m. when she got her kids up and ready to go to school and then herself ready to go to work. She and her second husband divide their time between homes in Seattle and Tucson.

Kay Kenyon has written six science fiction novels published by Bantam Books, as well as numerous short stories appearing in anthologies. Her early influences were teachers at the University of Washington, Roger Sale and Charles Johnson. She counts Robert Ray and Don McQuinn as inspirations, as well as her agent, Donald Maass. Her novels include *Tropic of Creation, The Braided World,* and *The Seeds of Time* (which won a prize in the PNWA Literary Contest in 1993). Her novel *Maximum Ice* was a finalist for the Phillip K. Dick Award, and has been translated into French. She has recently completed her most challenging novel to date, *Bright of the Sky*, the first of a quartet of books. She lives in Wenatchee, Washington, with her husband Tom Overcast.

Bharti Kirchner is a prolific author who has published eight books. Four of these are critically acclaimed novels. *Pastries: A Novel of Desserts and Discoveries, Darjeeling, Sharmila's Book*, and *Shiva Dancing*. Her books have been translated into German, Dutch, Spanish, Thai and other foreign languages. Winner of two Seattle Arts Commission literature grants and a GAP grant by Seattle's Artist Trust, Bharti also writes articles and essays for many national publications and anthologies, including book reviews for the *Seattle Times*. An award-winning cook, she is the author of four popular cookbooks, including *The Bold Vegetarian*.

Craig Lesley is the author of four novels and the editor of two short-story collections. He has received three awards from the Pacific Northwest Booksellers Association. *Winterkill* won both a PNBA award for Best Novel and the Golden Spur Award from the Western Writers of America for the Best Novel of 1984. Both *The Sky Fisherman* and *Storm Riders* were nominated for the Pulitzer Prize. Lesley has served as Hallie Ford Chair at Willamette University and Professor of Creative Writing at Whitman College. He is currently the Senior Writer-in-Residence at Portland State University. His work has earned him two grants from the National Endowment for the Humanities, a NEA Fellowship and a Bread Loaf Fellowship. *Burning Fence*, a nonfiction work about the rural West, is forthcoming from St. Martins' Press.

Mark Lindquist was born and raised in Seattle. He attended the University of Washington and University of Southern California. After graduating, he worked as a copy writer for a movie studio. His first novel, *Sad Movies*, was based on this brief experience. It became a bestseller for *Atlantic Monthly Press* and was published in six languages. Referred to by the press as one of the so-called "literary Brat Pack," he wrote screenplays, book reviews and articles, in addition to publishing his second novel, *Carnival Desires*, chronicling his Hollywood experience. Shortly thereafter he enrolled in Seattle University School of Law. He became a prosecuting attorney and spent five years in the Special Assault Unit. In 2000 *People Magazine* named him as one of the "100 Most Eligible Bachelors" in the country. That same year his third novel, *Never Mind Nirvana*, was published by Random House/Villard.

Don McQuinn determined to be a writer a year after retiring from the United States Marine Corps in 1970. It's possible he would have succeeded without the impetus provided by the Pacific Northwest Writers Association (known as the Pacific Northwest Writers Conference at the time), but the essential fact is that the impetus was provided, starting in 1971. He was fortunate enough to be accepted as a student in Zola Helen Ross's writing classes. The combination of her efforts and the critiques of other students established the foundation he's worked to build on ever since. His novels range from an examination of the Vietnam war through science fiction, have achieved best-seller status, and won the PNWA Achievement Award and the Governor's Award.

Fred Melton, is a full-time dentist from Wenatchee, Washington, whose writing has appeared in *Best American Mystery Stories 2002, Talking River Review, California Quarterly, Big Sky Journal, Northern Passages,* as well as other publications. His novel *Slough Creek* won second place in the 2004 PNWA Mainstream Novel Contest and the poems included in this anthology placed third.

Jim Molnar is a writer, editor and photographer currently at work on both fiction and nonfiction manuscripts. His several decades of work in daily journalism ranged from investigative and political reporting to news-feature writing and editing, including fifteen years with *The Seattle Times* travel section as a writer, editor and columnist. His travel journalism and photography, which has appeared in more than fifty newspapers, several anthologies and exhibitions, has merited a score of national and international awards. He's done some theater, written poetry with teens in juvenile detention, and works with other writers and authors as editor and coach. Jim, his family, and a cat called Enzo live in Seattle.

Marjorie Reynolds is an award-winning author. William Morrow & Co. published her novels, *The Starlite Drive-in* and *The Civil Wars of Jonah Moran*, in hardcover, and Berkley released them in paperback. The American Library Association chose *The Starlite Drive-in* as one of the Ten Best Books of 1998 for Young Adults, and Barnes & Noble selected it for a Discover Great New Writers Award. Rights were sold to seven countries. Her novels have received praise in the *New York Times, Kirkus, Publishers Weekly*, and *Booklist*, as well as in numerous other newspapers and publications. She teaches advanced fiction at the University of Washington Extension and conducts writing workshops in Washington, Oregon and California.

Ann Rule is regarded by many as the foremost true crime writer in America, and the author responsible for the genre as it exists today. She came to her career with a solid background in law enforcement and the criminal justice system. She has been a Seattle Policewoman, caseworker for the Washington State Department of Public Assistance, student intern at the Oregon State Training School for Girls. A full-time true crime writer since 1969, she has published twenty-four books, all *New York Times* bestsellers. To date, four of her books have been made into TV movies. She won the coveted Peabody Award for her miniseries, *Small Sacrifices*, and has two Anthony Awards from Bouchercon, the mystery fans' organization. She has been nominated four times for Edgar Awards from the Mystery Writers of America, and was also awarded the Washington State Governor's Award. Born in Lowell, Michigan, she now lives near Seattle, Washington, on the shores of Puget Sound. She is the mother of five, and grandmother of three.

Daniel Sconce says one of his first jobs out of junior college in Los Angeles was as the assistant to a Hollywood cameraman. It was 1972 and a good time to be a young man in the movie business. He was glad for the camera job and stayed with it for several years. After years of painting and writing for his own pleasure he began showing and selling his paintings in the late 1980s. Although his poems far outnumbered his paintings, he had no ambitions as a poet. Then in March of 2004, at the behest of his friend Kay Kenyon, he entered these poems in PNWA's Literary Contest. The result was winning the first place award. With the award money he self-published a collection of sixty-seven poems titled, *Becoming What It Will*.

Anna Sheehan was diagnosed with high-functioning autism at age eleven, and has been writing diligently since she learned how to type at the age of fourteen. She has found that writing enables her to understand the world better, and in understanding others, she can better understand herself. She mostly writes young adult fiction, aimed especially at teenagers with complicated lifestyles. At twenty-five she is currently working a farm in central Oregon, and raising her first child. She is a member of Wordos' critique group in Eugene, Oregon.

Indu Sundaresan is the author of two novels, *The Twentieth Wife* and *The Feast of Roses*, based on the life of the most powerful Empress in the Mughal dynasty that built the Taj Mahal in India. Her work has been translated into ten languages and she won the 2003 Washington State Book Award for *The Twentieth Wife*. Indu is currently working on a third novel, set in India in the 1940s.

Stephen John Walker was born and raised in Seattle, Washington. At age twenty-one, he entered the Army to "see the world." During the next thirty years his travels took him from the jungles of Central America and the highlands of South Vietnam to the fall of the Berlin Wall. Most of his stories are based on his personal experiences, or of those whom he met along the way. He now lives and writes just outside of Salem in the hills of western Oregon.

Shawn Wong's second novel, *American Knees*, was published by Simon & Schuster in 1995 (Scribner paperback, 1996). His first novel, *Homebase* (Reed and Cannon, 1979; reprinted by Plume/NAL, 1990), won both the Pacific Northwest Booksellers Award and the 15th Annual Governor's Writers Day Award of Washington. He is also the co-editor and editor of six Asian American and American multicultural literary anthologies including the pioneering anthology *Aiiieeeee! An Anthology of Asian American Writers* (Howard University Press, 1974; reprinted in four different editions, most recently by Meridian in 1997). He is currently Professor of English and Director of the University Honors Program at the University of Washington, where he previously served as Chair of the Department of English and Director of the Creative Writing Program. His poem, "Calling the Roll," included here was written for the University of Washington's "Day of Reflection and Engagement," October 11, 2001.

THE PEN AND THE KEY: *50th Anniversary Anthology of*
Pacific Northwest Writers was set in a variation of Bembo,
a text type noted for its classical beauty and readability.
Bembo was modeled on type cut by Francesco Griffo in
Venice, Italy, in 1495. It takes its name from its first use in
Aldus Manutius' printing of *De Aetna* by Pietro Bembo.
A standard typeface in Europe since its origin, Bembo was
redesigned for the Monotype Corporation in 1929, and
digitized in 1990 for Adobe Systems, Inc.

Printing of this book has been made possible through
the generosity of The Boeing Company,
printed by The Boeing Company in
Kent, Washington, USA,
on acid free paper.

Production by Rosemary Jones
Design by Victoria Sturgis
Cover art by Nicholas Wilton

74th Street Productions, LLC
350 North 74th Street, Seattle, Washington 98103
206-781-1447   www.74thstreet.com

Pacific Northwest Writers Association
www.pnwa.org